TITLE AND DEED

Will Eno

TITLE AND DEED

monologue for a slightly foreign man

OBERON BOOKS
LONDON

WWW.OBERONBOOKS.COM

First published in 2012 by Oberon Books Ltd
521 Caledonian Road, London N7 9RH
Tel: +44 (0) 20 7607 3637 / Fax: +44 (0) 20 7607 3629
e-mail: info@oberonbooks.com
www.oberonbooks.com

A catalogue record for this book is available from the British Library.

PB ISBN: 978-1-84943-480-5
EPUB ISBN: 978-1-84943-515-4

Cover image: Simon Larbalestier, 'Desert Storm 2001'.

Printed and bound by CPI Group (UK) Ltd, Croydon, CR0 4YY.

Visit www.oberonbooks.com to read more about all our books
and to buy them. You will also find features, author interviews and
news of any author events, and you can sign up for e-newsletters
so that you're always first to hear about our new releases.

To Gords, of Five Towns, and for Adrienne, of four, and to Houghtons, everywhere, and all the friends I'd be lost or worse without.

Characters

MAN

Title and Deed was first performed at The Alice Griffin Jewel Box Theatre on May 8 2012 with the following cast:

Man: **Conor Lovett**

Creative Team

Director: **Judy Hegarty Lovett**

Set Designer: **Christine Jones**

Costume Designer: **Andrea Lauer**

Lighting Designer: **Ben Stanton**

Production Stage Manager: **Donald Fried**

United States Premiere originally produced by Signature Theatre (James Houghton, Founding Artistic Director; Erika Mallin, Executive Director) in association with Gare St Lazare Players Ireland in the Alice Griffin Jewel Box Theatre at The Pershing Square Signature Center. Opening: May 20, 2012.

Signature Theatre is a not-for-profit organization founded in 1991 by James Houghton. The company exists to honor and celebrate the playwright. Signature makes an extended commitment to a playwright's body of work, and during this journey the writer is engaged in every aspect of the creative process. Signature is the first theatre company to devote an entire season to the work of a single playwright, including re-examinations of past writings as well as New York and world premieres. By championing in-depth explorations of a living playwright's body of work, Signature delivers an intimate and immersive journey into the playwright's singular vision.

Setting	the theater, a room
Characters	just a man; ideally, he is slightly foreign to his audience, though a native speaker of English
Wardrobe	simple, normal
Props	a bag or backpack containing a three-foot-long section of a wooden broomstick and a metal lunch box.

Lights up on MAN, just arriving in the middle of the stage, carrying a bag, which he sets down, at some point in the opening few lines.

MAN: I'm not from here. I guess I never will be. That's how being from somewhere works. I'll assume you are, though. That'll make everything make a little more, I think your word is, sense. And it might help to move things along. Let's hope. We don't need to hope. Things move quickly enough. In fact, we're practically almost done. It's my word, too, by the way, "sense." Oh, so, one other thing – don't hate me, if you wouldn't mind. Thanks. I know that's not something you can ask a person. But, you know, what is? So, yeah, don't walk out on me, or, if you do, try to walk out quietly. Keep the screaming to yourself, if you could, as we used to say back in the sand pits. Thanks. *(Small gesture towards bag.)* That's just a bag, by the way. Just some unattended luggage. No, seriously, don't worry, it's just my bag, a couple of belongings.

People don't gather enough, anymore. Where I'm from, we used to gather all the time – Midwinter's Eve, or for Reverse Weddings, or for something we had called Terrible Saturdays. So, yeah, thank you, and, welcome – it's nice to see a little clump.

Anyway, let's get back down to earth, to my arrival here, and I mean, just, here. The aeroporto, I think none of us calls it. Customs. I was one of the first people in the wrong line, and then someone helped me out, and I was suddenly the last person in the right one. And then, you've done this, through the zigzags, kicking the suitcase, and finally up to the welcome sign and bulletproof glass. I

remember my mouth suddenly getting dry
and my eyes starting to water, like I was about
to lie, even though I wasn't. Maybe other
people know that feeling? The truth in the
heart, the lump in the throat. "Business or
pleasure?," the man asked. "Neither," says I,
jauntily. "I'm here to save us all." "And who
is us?," he asked, writing. "Exactly," I said,
with a wink, though I would never wink and
jauntily's not the right word. The man looked
at me. "Seriously," he said. "Just visiting," I
said. "All right," he said. I believe I have that
verbatim. A number lit up over his head,
a nice six in your local governmental font.
"Business or pleasure," he said, to the next one
of me, some other version who'd just blown
in, full of hope and in the wrong clothes for
the climate, and I was on to the next line.
They scanned a photo of my retina. "Can I get

a copy of that," I said, "for a, you know, for
a keepsake?" They said, in the local parlance,
no. Then I was in. Then I was here. I don't
know why international travel puts me in such
a puckish mood. Maybe it's the free coffee
or the lack of sleep and oxygen. Maybe it's a
little hopeless glimmer of hope that I might
somehow, with a change of scenery, change.
Or the new bacteria, or, just, it's exciting.

Keepsake is a word we won't look into any
further, though I bet the right type of person
on the right lonely night could give himself
a pretty good cry by doing the etymology.
Or, herself. Trace the origin of any word and,
if you're half a man, and I can say without
bragging I am, or half a woman, which is sort
of my type, you'll shed some serious tears at
the long and trembling history of these frail
little sounds, made up out of nowhere. Lamp.

Horse. Shed. It's like loss and wandering and some strange German joy are built right in, somehow. They almost make you want to cry, or make you want to do something else, almost. Words. Ah, but they do the job. If you need a lamp or a horse. If you live in a shed and you're lost and trying to get home.

What next? Let me see. Let me stand here for a second and see.

The next part of my great voyage we can probably skip. It would just be different scenes of me in other lines, reading schedules, trying to get change, wishing I were home. Home where I'm from, that is, home where the hat's hanging and the placenta's buried. I doubt you've ever heard of it. Or, maybe some of you… *(Very brief pause, and he somewhat defensively moves on.)* No, I doubt

you have, and, of course, that's fine. It's just
a little thing, my country – down by the sea,
roughly, seasonal enough, a small population,
the chief exports sarcasm and uric acid. No,
but I'm proud of her, the old girl. The very
old woman. The lying-dying senile old mess,
so far away, her milky eyes trying to focus on
anything and her mouth opening and closing
for some reason other than to speak.

Maybe that's strange of me, to make a thing
into a person, and then to make the person
a weak and dying one. I don't know if I do it
out of love or one of the other feelings. Maybe
you're doing something similar, right now.
Making something into something else and
then somehow killing the second thing. Who
knows. I'm looking into your eyes and saying:
Who knows. It's scary but kind of interesting
to think the answer is: nobody. *(Brief pause.)*

The eyes are the window of the eyes. I'm
trying to remember who said that. *(Very brief
pause.)* It was a guy I used to paint houses
with. Brian.

Oh. Time to share. *(He gets the three-foot piece
of broomstick out of the bag.)* This is a nice
one of these, yeah? Maybe I'll play a little
something for you, later. I'm kidding – it's
not an instrument, it's just a stick, just one of
my belongings. A belonging of mine. I could
probably get a sound out of it, though.

*(Puts the stick back in the bag, or on top of
it, at some point in the next couple of lines.)* I
remember, back when I wasn't here, there was
always this thunder, this kind of, not really,
thunder, there. I don't know what that was.
Just always in the background, rolling, kind
of threatening, or soothing. For a long time I

thought it was inside my head. I could have asked. I don't know what they could've told me. But, anyway, thunder. A kind of steady beating, and a lot of rain, or a lot of gray skies, or a lot of blue skies under which we worried about rain. Anyway, the sky made so much noise I could never sleep, even as a child, even before that, even if it was in my head. I remember learning to read, late one rumbling night. My father came through the room to get a glass of water. "Don't move your lips," he said. "You're moving your lips." And that sound outside the house went on, or got a little louder. I know you have all that here, normal weather patterns and fathers walking through rooms and sound waves and so on. But it's different. The rain's not as rainy, or something, and the howl of my ancestors, or whatever that is, it sounds more like an ear infection, here, or some neurological thing.

Maybe this is progress, maybe that's what the world sounds like. Or maybe I'm romanticizing.

I don't want to paint too dreary a picture of the misery. Because I've laughed, in my life. In fact, on one particular full moon, I remember, I laughed until the sun came up, until things suddenly didn't seem that funny anymore. And I've been to the dances, the dances that anyone could go to, and I have supped at the…at the what? The table of something. I don't know how to finish that. *(A very small, quick, flourish.)* Olé.

Don't pity me, is all I'm saying, plus this, which is that I have loved, romantically. And, just as unbelievably, I've been loved.

And there can be no finer state. It's a many-splintered thing. Is that Shakespeare? Or, I just remembered, it was that same guy Brian. My thing is, I speak to you as a foreigner, yes, but also as a lucky person, as a recipient of one of the blessings our little planetarium can bestow. I assure you I'm here as a celebrant, tone and vocabulary aside. I have a sad way of talking, but that's just my voice. It's just the sound of my voice.

(Very brief pause.) We all have happy memories. We all have a funny little map in our head that divides the world into home and away.

There's a tradition, where I'm from, something started by the elders, a beautiful institution, maybe you have it here, where, having settled on your intended, you sit outside the window,

or the door, or at the end of the street, and
you wait, and you do not move. Maybe you
flinch from time to time, or you wince here
and there, because why wouldn't you wince,
but mainly you stay still and wait. You sit
and daydream and make plans in your head,
plans for your future happiness. Then the time
comes for you to move. Here, the tradition
insists you go and get the saddest instrument
you don't know how to play. Most people
reach for the cello, given the difficulty and
mournfulness of it, but I chose instead, when
it was my time, a tuba. I weighed less, when
I was courting Lauren, and needed the extra
heft. No, I probably weighed the same, but I
may have felt less – God, what did I feel less
of? – less landlocked? I doubt that describes it.
That doesn't describe it. Anyway, then, in our
tradition, you would play, on this instrument

you didn't know how to play, you would play

a song, something like a song, your love call,

so to speak, so that your intended could hear

the sound of your desire, untutored and new,

unpracticed, authentic, poor, true. And then

she would try to sing along to whatever awful

noise was being made. It all makes a kind of

sense, if you have a feeling for what makes

people tick, and not tick. Spring nights, when

the frogs are beginning to thaw, and everyone

is falling in love, our little part of creation

sounds like the happiest, worst orchestra in

the world, tuning up. The women, often

women, usually women, would lean out the

windows and try to make mistakes in perfect

time with their men. And this is how life went

on. How the species noisily stayed a species.

Joy, eternal – until the mating season ended.

And after that, it was all downhill, but it felt

like all uphill, but in reality, in another reality, it was probably flat, probably just a different kind of joyous. Lauren and I saw eye to eye for a while, but we were not to be, so I went my separate ways.

But, God. Our feelings, back there, back home, what a racket they made. All those rented instruments and leaning women. I miss it. You must have it here, some similar, I don't know, a similar pageantry and din. Not in my experience, but my experience here is very limited. Probably you have something else that works fine. It does seem quiet, though. I haven't noticed a lot of wailing or keening or screaming, around here. Maybe I've fallen in with the wrong crowd. *(Very brief pause.)* I don't mean you, I mean, in real life.

Sorry, if I'm…yeah.

We were taught not to talk about love. In fact, while we were indoors, we were encouraged to keep quiet on a whole range of topics. We had some different ideas about human life and the rearing of it, but we liked to think, at the very least, that our eyes were open. Which they often were. Although, I could be imagining things. Maybe I'm just imagining we had traditions and ways of life. But I don't think I am. I believe my life happened. I'm thinking of a night in the cemetery with Lauren. Her teeth in the moonlight, a pebble pressed into her elbow, all that dewy actuality. Our eyes were open. I like the little narrow roads they have in there. All the old names that look so old they seem foreign. Lauren smiled. No birds, quiet moon. True story.

But, don't get the wrong idea. We weren't all muddy skies and weeping and fornicating in the gravel. We were good at sports. Or, not sports, exactly. But, we had a national bird and special days when everything was closed. I think every country has a Memorial Day, has War Dead to honor, or some bright moment when the nation was born. Ours fell in September, and the custom was you had to make bread for anyone who asked. We were a good people, us. I like to think I'm a good person. I mean, not deep down.

We used to always…yeah, I'm sure we used to always do something. *(Brief pause. To someone in the audience.)* Sorry. I thought I saw a look in your eyes and started thinking.

I'm sorry – you can't believe how far away I feel. The answer is far. Count yourself lucky to have a safe and warm Point A somewhere in your past. I imagine myself striking out into the world, one foot in the grave, the other in my mouth, and how's anyone supposed to walk like that? Or, I imagine myself with my reading glasses resting on my forehead, as I travel the world, continent after continent, storming through cities and fields, looking for my glasses. I think that's very human of me. Near-sighted in one country is near-sighted in the next. I don't know how I imagine myself, honestly. Maybe slightly taller, with different insides. Or swinging in a hammock, on a little piece of land, without heart trouble of any kind.

But, again, I sound so dour, and I'm not. I mean, look at me. *(Brief pause, in which he stands still.)* Thanks. But, no, I knew how to unwind, back home. In fact, I could unwind almost completely. I'd chew on a piece of pine fruit and stare at the stars, almost completely unwound. Or I'd sit behind the house and try to hyperventilate or throw my bike down a hill or draw my veins on my arms and legs. I kept busy, is my point. It wasn't all scarring, back when the days weren't as numbered and bedtime was for pretending to sleep. I had a pony, almost, twice, and there was always a roof over my head to go up and sit on. And, you probably wouldn't believe it to look at me, but there'd even be the odd night when I'd enjoy a warm skipplejick. *(Brief pause, waiting for a response.)* Do you not call them that here? The point is, I'm not here to complain. I'm merely noting differences, registering differences, in an effort to draw my blurry homeland into a little more focus, so that I might decide to homesickly set sail, or happily stay put here forever. Maybe you're at a similar point in your trajectory. On the transom, or

at a fork in the road, right in the middle of
the tail end of a little lucky streak. That's an
odd euphemism for the life span, trajectory,
but it has the right connotations, the human-
cannonball feel at the beginning, the sickening
thump at the end. Good morning, world;
maybe I should be a veterinarian or an
oceanographer; maybe I'll marry a princess;
thump.

But, what else? In terms of facts. Who else?
I'm shooting for the essential, here. Mothers
and Fathers? Those are something we probably
share. We bury our mothers and fathers with
tears in our eyes, back home. This is universal,
I think, the burying, and fairly common,
the tears. My ma and pa were sometimes
known…wait. *(He opens and closes his mouth
several times.)* Sorry, did you hear that? My
jaw is…it's making a noise. *(Opens and closes*

mouth.) Did you… *(Once more.)* I guess it's
gone. No, there it is. I think the words take
a toll. They sort of wear you down, certain
sounds, as they move past. "Past." But I
wouldn't trade them for anything, words. No,
actually, I would. I would, but, for what, and
with whom?

So, no, it's probably not easy. To show up, as
I've shown up, on your alien shore, here, with
most of the holidays being different, and the
few parades we share not looking the same.
We, God, back there, we'd throw a parade for
anything. Shortest day of the year, longest,
some kid got his braces off, another kid got
scratched by a cat. We were nothing, if we
were not festive. Even a neighbor's domestic
dispute had us dusting off the bass drum and
making banners that said, "Communication is
so important." I think we just loved to march

and take a stab at music. And why wouldn't we. Life was essentially a parade and it would only stop to let the ambulance through.

I don't know if you've ever followed an ambulance with your mother in it. It's mainly like driving a car, and you only start to cry when they stop running red lights or turn the siren off. The whole time you're wondering, "Does this have to happen and, since it does, does it have to happen like this?" It really doesn't matter what you scream, so scream what you like, scream your head off, son. Daughter. They're ahead of you in another vehicle and can't hear you anyway.

I once was…nah, I probably never was. I probably never was. *(Brief pause.)* What a moment, I suddenly seem to have here, with you. Standing here, a homesick orphan fuck,

with no map, compass, food, bed, love. No,
I don't suppose it's very easy for me. Nor for
you. Alas, you know. God's wounds. And is
this the part where I suddenly say, "you know,
we're not that different, you and I"? I don't
think so. It's probably where I say: if you have
nothing good in your heart, as I don't, and
nothing good in your head, as I don't, then it
doesn't matter if you're out in the back yard
or across the coldest ocean, you are and will
always be, away from home, not at home.
Not homeless, per se, necessarily, but, un-
homed. Made-up word. What word isn't. Not
important. People give them a hard time, but,
words are fine, as said earlier, they do the trick.
"My horse is sick." "Hand me that lamp." I
make these sounds and someone understands,
someone comprehends, and they hand me a
lamp or destroy my horse. Which is a miracle,

sense and meaning, feeling, that we get across
even a tenth of it. And, I'm not even from
here. Though we all share an origin that is,
essentially, wordless. Prior to the flood and the
word "flood." We all come from blood and
salt water and a screaming mother begging for
us to leave. And this must be an early piece
of learning, something we carry with us for
all time, eternal, that our arrival here caused
a terrible and unsayable pain, such that all
that any of the participants in that miraculous
moment could do was scream. Just scream
and scream, no words in sight, nothing to put
a period on. No, there was nothing on the
walls of the hospital where I was born. None
of the advertising or posters about choking
that you've got. There was a mirror, though,
in the birthing room. I swear I remember
it. The industrial floor tile and the whole

interior. The doctor said, "It's a boy." There's a way of saying that, where, depending on the delivery, it can sound more like a diagnosis than a piece of news. And then, there was this moment, maybe even caught in the mirror, of silence and peace, just mother and child and sunlight, where I swear the whole thing could be sensed, the plain truth, that this is not forever, no part of this is for forever, and all we had to do, after we'd dutifully done our screaming, all we humans in that room had to do, to begin an endless series of endings and departures and emigrations and amazement, was keep breathing. In and out, for as long as we could. The light was just right, for a moment like that. Slanty and golden. My mother said, "There, there," and, in retrospect, she was probably right. It wasn't a sad or dark or downward moment, it was just very heavily

true. Then my father walked in with a balloon,
though this I only know from a photograph.
They were good people, them, but they're
dead to me now, both having died. The father
first, as nature would have it, and the mother
later and in greater pain, and is that, again,
as nature would have it? Poor women. It just
doesn't stop, does it? Bleeding and bleeding
and then that stops and it's "Goodnight
Irene," if your name is Irene and it's night
when you die. There's something sadder about
a woman dying than a man. There's something
sad about it all, about both. I just happen
to have gotten most of my shelter from
the former, so any tenderness tends in that
direction.

(Brief pause.) What's that stuff you serve on
salad, here? I've never seen it before. Some
kind of root or something? I just was looking

through a window at a woman who had a pile
of whatever it is on her plate. She touched it
with a fork and tried to smile. They came by
and took the other silverware away. I don't
know if there was music playing.

Yeah, sorry, but, I don't sense much joy,
around here, with all of you. Maybe it's there,
and I don't know how to read it. Maybe it's
all you feel, and I can only see it as something
else.

But, again, I don't mean to judge. I'm just very
far from the comforting things, as you may
be. And in this state, as you may know, you
can see with some precision the long straight
line. All of us marching out of the ocean,
breathing and breathing and breathing, and
then dropping dead on land, on some land
we like to mistakenly think of as ours. Thank

God, I guess, that we invented words to huff and puff, to give the whole thing some shape. There's a school of thought that says loneliness evolved sometime around the larynx, not long after the thumb. Maybe it's no surprise there isn't more smiling, but I still find it surprising.

(Pause. Looks around in audience for a smile. Finds one.) There we go. Very nice. Don't ever change. Or, if you like, change.

When I got here, about two months ago in human months, I fell in with a family, name of Miller. He did construction; she, a nurse; the girl was in school; and the boy, barely an infant, just cried and cried, and who would hold it against him, other than his parents or anyone else with a problem with littleness. They were smiley people. You could call them one of my chances. The arrangement was I'd help out around the house, but I didn't, so they asked me to leave, and I left, goodbye to the Millers. They taught me important lessons, in that brief time, mainly lessons about how to live with the Millers, but I hope to somehow extrapolate. I won't soon forget them, unless I'm thinking of the Muellers, who I didn't like at all. No, it was the Millers, and they were wonderful people. They took me in and tried to make me feel at home, having never been there, but at least they took guesses. One night, I came home and there was a tree branch in my bed. Don't know what that meant, exactly, but I'm sure it's a meaningful tribute somewhere. It's a shame. I wasn't a gracious guest, and I'm sure this deprived them of their chance to be gracious hosts. Although, I did cut my foot on a rusty metal stair, the morning I was leaving, and they tried to be understanding and said I should clean it.

I don't know if my voice sounds funny? I was using it a lot, last night. Screaming at traffic, or something. Or it might be allergies. And I wasn't really raised to speak indoors. Causation – go figure it. And I probably haven't been sleeping. Not to fall back on a favorite refrain, but: who knows. *(To a woman.)* You look like you might. Maybe? All right.

I've had occasion – this is embarrassing – to question my existence, just the plainest fact of it. Not in big ways, just little constant daily ones. This might be something the folks instilled in me. Bless their hearts, they loved me like only they could: out of the corners of their eyes, kind of, and with penetrating questions like, "Who exactly do you think you are?" and "And now where do you think you're going?" I miss my mom and dad, whoever I am, whatever's wrong with me.

But the Millers were nice. They seemed very much "from here." Just very solidly present. Which is all I'm really aiming for, right now. And so questions of here or there are hardly the point, except to further define the notion of the present moment, and actual life, as we do and don't know it, and so my problem of having one foot somewhere and the other somewhere else is really neither here nor there and should only be seen as the identification of two distant points, so as to triangulate a third and more vivid possibility. You could call this an existential crisis or dilemma, but it's really more just that my stomach hurts and I want someone to put their hand on my neck and say, "It'll be all right. We'll get you home."

No, I'm okay.

(Brief pause.) I should have brought water. My throat's drying out.

(Brief pause.) I met a blonde woman, the other – I don't know – the other week. She was from here, like yourselves. From this, this sounds so sexual, vicinity. She had a pretty way of cringing and nice blue eyes. She worked with the deaf. I found that interesting. Sometimes, she'd bring them a kitten. When I asked her why, she said, "They're cute." She was good for the world. Her life…well, I guess the word would be value, her life has value. It counts.

The world. I have these things, these words I return to. The world, women, animals, men, heart defects, disabilities, trying. My themes. The syllables I return and return to. "So, you like repeating yourself?" you say.

"I like repeating myself," I say. Because, you know, who else is going to do it? Who else is going to ride my personality into the ground and wring the last ounce of words out of my head? Others? Yeah, that's true, actually – I guess others could do it. But that doesn't mean I shouldn't try to get the most out of the old girl, which is how I refer to my body, strangely. I don't, really, I guess. But I don't call it a Him, either. It's an it, as yours is. Think, for instance, of Leonardo da Vinci or Joan of Arc. Think of Genghis Khan, or Novak Djokovic. Think of all the bodies, the muscled and rippled and lithesome Its that once strode the wonderful Earth, sailed the seventy seas, coughing and wheezing and theorizing and sinking. The magnificent Its, come and gone, neither hither nor yon. It's exciting, isn't it. Being a part of the great

Hide-and-Seek? The great swarm, the living
billions, as we try to get our footing, place
ourselves in some continuum, before the
lights go out and the thing discontinues. It's
exciting, if nothing else. Now you see us,
oh my God I can't breathe, now you don't.
And then we're all by the grave in the rain,
dreaming of breakfast. "He was a good man,
even a family man, in his way. But, not
anymore. Now he's in a coffin, or across the
river, or in the clouds. And wherever he is, we
pray his soul might find repose, that it might
find rest, somewhere, at least for a while, if not
for ever and ever, Amen."

(Brief pause.) That was a eulogy. Everything is,
if you have a good sense of humor, a positive
mindset. I mean that. If you have the right
attitude, the right kind of bright and cheerful
approach, the whole fucking swill-hole is just a

long line of informative and beautiful funerals.
Here comes one now. I can almost see it, as it
disappears. *(He closes his eyes.)* The steam rising
off the sweating horses in the winter weather.
Their breath, visible. The quiet, the sound of
wooden cart wheels on a cobbled road. You, in
tears, or dead. The smell of worms and roots,
the smell of cold air. *(He opens his eyes.)* Can
you picture it? Something close? Something
ceremonious? Flowers and dirt and the whole
crying family. The landscapers smoking. The
folding of the death rug and a bottle of pine
sap broken over the coffin. The speechlessness.
The survivor's veiny hands.

I'm describing my own, how we have
them back home. Hence the horses and
cobblestone, which, when I think of it, we
don't have anymore. I'm also describing it
from the perspective of the living. Which is

how we tend to see everything. We're very living-oriented, aren't we. This is how a funeral might seem to the deceased. *(He holds a long, tense, pause. Mumbles something urgently but quietly, indecipherably. Then, a very quiet but menacing drone. Then one small sad sound.)* *(Brief pause.)* No, that's probably not right. *(Brief pause.)* We have a tradition, where I hail from, of crying. Late at night, broad daylight, whenever we have a moment. I'm sure you do too. But, we really made a name for ourselves with it. But I swear that I am, like you, not unhappy.

(Brief pause.) We should thank our stars, if we believe in stars, for the listeners of the world. You're doing fine, is what I'm saying. You're doing very well and I thank you.

The blonde woman had a nice name: Lisa. It's good, yeah? It doesn't really preen, as a name. Lisa, you remember, from the vicinity? She tried to take me to a Trivia Night, for a taste of the local culture. It was a good idea, but we went on the wrong night. Do you know what night is Trivia Night at the Whately Cafe? Wednesday, the correct answer is Wednesday. But so we walked around for a while. It was cold and supposed to snow. So that was something we shared, that it was supposed to snow.

You don't see much ice or snow where I'm from. I do have a story, though, a sighting. I could never sleep, whatever year I'm thinking of, and so was out, at some ungodly hour, on some bastardly late winter night, taking my walk. It was only me, or farmers, or escapees or hunters, who were out in the very cold dark. I could hear that thundery sound I was always hearing, although it sounded more metallic. I stopped to turn around and then turned around again. And then I saw the sight it seemed I was born to see, if I was born for a reason. The scene was this, in words, it was about a hundred just-shorn sheep, shorn too early in the season, standing dead still, all facing the same way, with a couple of skinny cows mixed in, standing as still as the sheep, and then the snow beginning to slowly fall. Silent scrawny creatures in the slow-motion snow, a communal shiver that would make its way through the crowd, an occasional animal vowel sound, and that was quietly all, that was quietly that.

It was there, standing before all them huddled against the weather, that I decided to leave, for real and for good, and not just in my heart.

And not just leave there, but try to actually go somewhere. I thought, "Maybe I've been adapting to the wrong surroundings." It wasn't a moment I fully understood, though there was definitely a strain of hope in it. Maybe another decade or two went by, and, ta-da. Je suis arrivé. That's French. Or, according to earlier claims, it's a eulogy. If everything is. I guess "Here we are" announces the death of our having been somewhere else. Who knows, again, and so on. The leafless trees, against the winter sky. The breath, visible. And so on. Words are all right. You say what you want, at the end of the day, they somehow work their magic. "Please stay seated." *(Very brief pause. No one has moved.)* See? Thank you. Well done. "Remain forever lost, ye beautiful and crooked people, wandering in the wilderness of doubt." *(Very brief pause.)* Again, wow, well done. Very nicely done.

Electricity, let's talk about that. It varies.
Different regions, different plugs and voltages.
Let's not talk about that. Let's try to stick to
the things that don't vary. But what doesn't
vary?

(Brief pause.) I wasn't breast-fed. So I didn't
really know what to reach for or something.
Maybe I should've said that, at the beginning.
I found my mother's diary, is how I know,
although I also had a feeling, if that's what that
was. The top of the baby bottle I originally
drank from got lost at some point, the part
with the rubber nipple, so I, apparently,
would kind of lap the baby-formula from
this wide-mouthed pickle jar they'd put near
me on the ground. It was a sight, my mother
wrote, that, quote, "did not fill anyone with
much pride." There's a later entry about my
father not being very happy about my teeth

coming in. Something about him not liking the consonant sounds I started making. The same day he said that, we, reportedly, drove somewhere to look at a dining room table someone was giving away. I was in the back seat, looking out the window, staring fearfully at the world and smiling, reportedly.

Somebody told me, I think it was a nutritionist I met, that you have to have a bicycle when you're little. That it's the law here. That can't be true, can it? True or false, it's a beautiful idea. *(To the audience in general.)* Remember, that night, years ago, when you were a beautiful idea? When you were just a glint and a smirk and an unspecified word? *(Very brief pause.)* Of course not – you weren't there. Except in spirit. In the spirit of a word or a smirk.

Lisa and I were going to rent a tandem once. It was just that kind of day. Lisa, I've mentioned her a few times now, she of the blondeur. I had the wrong identification or something, so they wouldn't let us take one, but we watched everyone else. I remember, there was a mother with her daughter, in unmatching outfits, trying to patch things up somehow, wobbling off together. Lisa looked disappointed but pretty, sitting there watching. I just remembered this: bangs. Bangs? That's some thing with how you wear your hair, yeah? I'd never heard that until I heard it from her. She was an education, our Lisa. One time, we went to a flea market and she told me, "Don't get too lost for too long," while she was flipping through some used post cards. That was a good day.

I think she couldn't handle the distance. I mean, the distance of me, or something. She asked me, very innocently, what I was doing on Earth. She said, "It's all right, if you're not sure." She straightened my collar and said, "You look like you just got born. Most people get over that. I could hold you," she said. I remember because it was memorable. "I could hold you." She would've been a good person to tremble with. But I got stupid and cold, and probably left her no choice. She was sweet when she ended it. She said, "You're really not where I see myself in five years." I don't know if she worked on that for days or just said it off the top of her head. I had hopes that we, that she and I... I just thought we'd exist for a while. She dropped off some things I'd left at her house, along with a calendar with all the days we'd spent together blacked out. Is that something people do? Is there something people don't? You know? It's such a range.

I'd like to think it was her loss, but sometimes it's hard to tell which loss is whose. I never really knew where I stood, with Lisa and everyone and all that.

The fucking world. I'm sorry, but, the fucking earth. Time, place, happiness. A person should be able to figure it out. It's only three things. Where did Philosophy go? Or Religion? We've had ten thousand years of people telling us what life is and how best to live it as it quickly goes by. And what has it given us? Me? I hope not. I don't know. Maybe homesickness and seasickness are the new and improved way of feeling at home. Or, maybe…just, anything.

God, water. *(Brief pause.)* They say to touch the roof of your mouth with your tongue.

(Brief pause, as he does so.) It's just a bad patch. I'm all right. I'm not feeling anything you haven't felt. It's like, you know, when they have you gargle with the sand for your second birthday. *(He turns away, momentarily, sees his bag. He gets the old metal lunchbox out of the bag.)* This'll offer us a little diversion. A little breather. My other belonging. Now, this object tells an interesting story. *(He holds it up for a moment.)* Not in words, I guess. *(He opens it. It's empty.)* Ah. The universe provides. I mean it. There's room to put something in there. *(Sets it down or puts it back in the bag, somewhere in the next few lines.)* I travel light. Or I don't have very much. By way of explanation.

(Referring to any piece of jewelry or any kind of accessory that someone in the audience is wearing.) I'm noticing your thing, there.

Where I'm from, at least in the western part,
you have a birth cloud. They take you out
the day you're born, the day after, and you all
look up, and you pick a cloud, and if some
uncle has a camera he takes a picture, and
that's your birth cloud, and there you are. In
the old days, they used to do a drawing. Good
tradition, The Birth Cloud. It was to remind
us, I guess, of what happens, eventually. It was
nice, whatever it meant, a comfort, whatever
the ancient roots. I'm sure you have something
similar, here. I know you have the Birth
Stone. That's obviously very different, but
somehow a similar statement is being made.
"You're a deaf and mute block of matter" or,
"You're drifting by and slowly disappearing."
Something like that. A little fact to put around
the child's neck to guide him or her in his or
her behavior.

(Without making any sounds, he opens and closes his mouth several times.) Sorry, again, but, you must hear that? No? Sorry. I grind my teeth in my sleep. I guess I grind them when I'm up, too.

(Brief pause.) I don't have a relative anywhere on this continent. Maybe you find that comforting.

(He works his mouth, for just a second, perhaps gags, for a second.) This doesn't feel good. But, we came here to get somewhere.

We actually have a word, "somewhere." And a word, "nowhere." We have a word, "tree," too, but you can actually picture that. I guess there was a need. I guess it was important we had names for places, even if we didn't have the places.

(Brief pause.) Before my father died, he didn't have a lot left of the gifts that you, again, thank you kindly and sincerely, are currently lavishing on me. Meaning, mainly, hearing and seeing. I'd say, "You want some cheese and crackers?" and he'd say, "Watch your mouth." So I'd say: *(Mumbles an indecipherable short sentence, something like: "Get your own fucking lunch," but indecipherable.)* In the end, his world was just a room, and a window, and the walk out to the mailbox. The world gets very small, doesn't it, penultimately. I wasn't by his side or anything, at the exact moment. I'm told he had no last words, just some different sounds. I was asleep, or just waking up. Time Zones, you know. And so ended his great journey, reportedly.

Lavishing is the word. I do thank you.

(Somewhere in the following lines a very gentle and imperceptible light shift should begin to occur, resulting in the "nice glow" that's referred to in the end.) I made it back for my mother's, though. The words very close to her dying words were "How is Catherine?" I think she thought I was her cousin. "Was there any traffic?" she asked me. Women care more about the world, so it's bigger for them, and maybe that's why it's sadder when they die. My mother said, "Tell them not to have a parade," because she never liked the mess. Then she said, "I can see you." She put her hands in front of her face. "Where's the little person?" And then she said, "Flowers would've brightened things up." And then her breathing changed and then because of fluid that had built up, or, just, it doesn't matter why, just, suddenly, she wasn't, I don't know how to say

it, she wasn't my mother anymore. But she still was. Her breathing got very raspy, or, some adjective. She died, would be the most economical way to put it. Where do you look, in the room? Where do you stand? No corner is corner enough, in certain rooms.

(Brief pause.) I'm sorry. We've all lost someone, I'm sure, someone who held us down to earth somehow or pointed us off in the right direction. I say this gently, and maybe it's just the light, but, God, we all look like we've got barely anyone left. *(Very brief pause.)* I'm sorry about that. All those losses. Each with its own, I don't know, dimensions? Co-ordinates? It's disorienting. What do you do. Where do you turn.

(A little lost in a sad and painful reverie of loss, he takes out the three-foot piece of broomstick.)

This is made out of electrons. Ash, actually. I think it's ash. I've kept it all these years. *(He gently taps several times the side of his lower leg. Then he strikes his leg very hard, "whack.")* Hey, still works. *(He hits himself again, twice, and then, again, several more times. Perhaps in tears.)* That's for the things I don't know. That's for all the places. *(Another whack or two.)* The old song and dance. The old girl. I'm sorry.

(Long pause. He regains a kind of raw but simple composure.) I've gotten sidetracked. I was talking about travel and how it started with my mother and father. They brought me into this world, of course, and taught me the difference between right and left. They taught me the word home, the word walk. *(He looks at someone in the audience. Gently.)* What's that look? *(Very brief pause.)* No, it's nice.

I had wanted to leave you with something.
(Very brief pause. Seeming to respond to an audience member's anxiety.) I know, I know, time, of course – I'm sure we all have somewhere we're supposed to be. *(Brief pause.)* There's a nice little glow, here. Is that…am I seeing that right? It's sort of morning-like? Late morning?

Don't get too lost for too long. They stop looking, eventually. Then even you forget you were ever out here somewhere.

(Another brief moment of difficulty, with breathing, swallowing, the jaw, etc.) This might be a good place to stop. Here.

It's a funny thing, it's strange – thirst, or whatever this is. Being a person. All the needs, the feelings, all the different things arising,

thoughts. *(Lights begin a five second fade.)* The
Earth.

End.

OTHER WILL ENO TITLES

Middletown

ISBN 9781849430661

Oh, the Humanity and other good intentions

ISBN 9781840028324

Thom Pain (based on nothing)

ISBN 9781840024524

The Flu Season

ISBN 9781840023701

Tragedy: a tragedy

ISBN 9781840022346

WWW.OBERONBOOKS.COM

Follow us on www.twitter.com/@oberonbooks
& www.facebook.com/oberonbook

First published in the United States by
Lonely Planet Global Limited
www.lonelyplanetkids.com

First published in the United Kingdom by
Quarto Publishing plc in 2018

2018 2019 2020 2021 / 10 9 8 7 6 5 4 3 2 1

ISBN: 978-1-78701-804-4

This book was conceived, designed and produced by
The Bright Press, an imprint of The Quarto Group
The Old Brewery
6 Blundell Street
London, N7 9BH
United Kingdom
T(0)20 7700 6700 F(0)20 7700 8066
www.quartoknows.com

Publisher: Mark Searle
Associate Publisher: Emma Bastow
Creative Director: James Evans
Art Director: Katherine Radcliffe
Managing Editor: Isheeta Mustafi
Senior Editor: Caroline Elliker
Project Editors: Alison Morris, Abi Waters
Design: Ali Adlington, Nina Tara

Printed and bound in the UAE

MIX
Paper from
responsible sources
FSC
www.fsc.org
FSC® C004800

UNOFFICIAL
LEGO® PROJECTS
TO BUILD!

BRICK CITY

LONDON

Warren Elsmore

lonely planet

Contents

There are 20 projects in this book to make yourself. Just look out for the brick symbol.

Welcome to Brick City
London

Read all about it! Read all about it! Come on up me old china plate (mate!) and welcome to one of the most iconic cities in the world—London. It's survived floods, fires, plagues, and bombings and still come out on top. Londoners are made of tough stuff, just like the pigeons that flutter and bob along the busy streets. There's enough innovation to put a crackle in the air but it never drowns out a story of times gone by. Grand monuments stand alongside glowing West End theaters, charming cafés, and a headline-grabbing royal family—and their palace.

Brick City London will take you on a whistle-stop tour of the city's most iconic attractions, from the Houses of Parliament to its handsome red phone boxes. Check out the amazing LEGO® models and scratch your head in wonder while you imagine the scent of frying fish and chips and the sound of Camden's punk rockers.

Want to know Big Ben's real name? How to become a Wimbledon ball girl/boy? Read on and discover plenty of fun facts along the way. And you don't have to be a master builder to get involved.

Brick City London includes easy-to-follow instructions for 20 fun, unofficial LEGO® projects that you can make yourself.

Hold the city in the palm of your hand, from a fire-breathing City of London dragon to a cute red bus. Our expert author will guide you through the process, with tips on LEGO® building and sourcing unusual bricks. The Big Smoke awaits. Go and get stuck in!

TURN OVER TO SEE ALL THE BUILDABLES!

Brick Builds

Here's a quick visual guide to all the buildable LEGO® models in this book

REMEMBER! IF YOU SEE ME YOU CAN MAKE IT!

RED PHONE BOX PAGE 12

BOWLER HAT PAGE 16

ORB PAGE 34

STOCKS PAGE 39

10 DOWNING STREET PAGE 24

RAVEN PAGE 36

QUEEN'S GUARDS PAGE 64

THE CORONATION CHAIR PAGE 47

CITY OF LONDON DRAGON PAGE 53

FISH & CHIPS PAGE 79

THE BRITISH MUSEUM
PAGE 72

RED BUS PAGE 104

SHERLOCK HOLMES
PAGE 123

CHINATOWN PAGE 92

FOOD TRUCK PAGE 84

ABBEY ROAD PAGE 106

WIMBLEDON
PAGE 113

LORD'S CRICKET
GROUND PAGE 111

UNDERGROUND TRAIN
PAGE 100

CANAL BOAT PAGE 118

TATE MODERN

The Tate Modern is one of London's most amazing spaces. Believe it or not, the main building used to be Bankside Power Station. Built using 4.2 million bricks and 656 feet- (200m-) long, the Swiss architects Herzog and de Meuron scooped the prestigious Pritzker Architecture Prize for transforming the empty power station. The echoey Turbine Hall entrance showcases changing art installations by famous artists, from giant swings and slides, to a crunchy carpet of ceramic sunflower seeds for visitors to walk over.

More than 60,000 works are on constant rotation at Tate Modern. The curators have famous works by Henri Matisse, Mark Rothko, Jackson Pollock, and Damien Hirst all at their fingertips!

SPEEDY HUNTERS

Peregrine falcons are the fastest creatures on the planet. When they dive to attack their prey they can reach an incredible 199 mph (320km/hr). They like open spaces and cliffs, but they occasionally decide to live on city buildings. A few have chosen the Tate Modern as a place to hang out.

SOMETIMES BIRDWATCHERS SET UP OUTSIDE WITH THEIR BINOCULARS, HOPING FOR A PEREGRINE PEEK.

Red Phone Box

There's a surprising secret behind London's iconic red phone booths. Sir Giles Gilbert Scott, who first designed them in 1924, was inspired by the grave of architect Sir John Soane and his family in a churchyard in St. Pancras. Scott used the tomb shape as a model for his booths, which were painted red to make them easy to spot.

Nowadays they only survive in conservation areas where they are often surrounded by crowds of selfie-happy tourists. Some have been sold and repurposed as cafés, libraries, and even mobile phone repair shops. Modern replacement "booths" have high-speed wi-fi and touch-screen journey planners.

DEATH OF A PHONE BOOTH

A bent and shattered phone box appeared in Soho in 2006, lying sadly on the pavement with a pickaxe in its middle and a wound "bleeding" red paint. It wasn't the victim of a phone box psychopath, however—this was guerrilla art by graffiti artist Banksy.

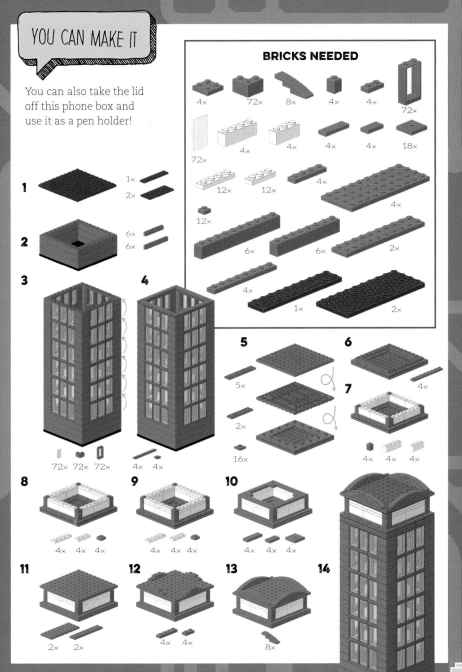

YOU CAN MAKE IT

You can also take the lid off this phone box and use it as a pen holder!

BRICKS NEEDED

4× 72× 8× 4× 4× 72×

72× 4× 4× 4× 4× 18×

12× 12× 4×

12×

6× 6× 2×

4×

1× 2×

1 1× 2×

2 6× 6×

3 **4**

72× 72× 72× 4× 4×

5 **6**

5× 4×

7

2×

16× 4× 4× 4×

8 **9** **10**

4× 4× 4× 4× 4× 4× 4× 4× 4×

11 **12** **13** **14**

2× 2× 4× 4× 8×

THE GLOBE THEATER

TO BE, OR NOT TO BE...

Britain's most famous playwright, William Shakespeare, lived and worked in London roughly 400 years ago. One of the theaters where his plays were performed was the Globe, which stood on the southern bank of the River Thames. Today there's a modern reconstruction close to the original site. The cheapest tickets are for the "groundlings," who stand in front of the stage.

NO FAKES

Shakespearean actors used props such as real swords, which could cause nasty accidents onstage. In a stage fight actors wore sheeps' bladders filled with animal blood under their costumes, ready to give the illusion of a mortal wound.

LADS IN DISGUISE

Women weren't allowed on stage in Shakespeare's time, so the female parts were played by boys. There was stiff competition for the best parts, but once they grew and their voices broke, there was no guarantee they could carry on.

PANTS ON FIRE

In 1613, the Globe went up in
flames during a performance of
Shakespeare's Henry VIII. A cannon
used as a prop misfired, setting fire to
the roof. Nobody was hurt except a
man who had to put out his burning
breeches with a bottle of ale!

Each stage pillar is
a whole oak tree.
Over 1,000 were
used to build the
new Globe.

BOWLER HAT

Welcome to 1950s London where businessmen wearing bowler hats flow over London Bridge every morning. Founded in the capital in 1765, Lock & Co is the oldest hat shop in the world and even makes headgear by royal appointment. Lock & Co was the original inventor of the bowler hat, or "Coke" (pronounced "cook"). It was designed in 1849 as a commission for nobleman Edward Coke who wanted to protect his gamekeeper's (a person in charge of animals on a private estate) heads from low-hanging branches when they were riding. Since then they have made bowlers for many famous customers, from Sir Winston Churchill to Charlie Chaplin.

In the James Bond film *Goldfinger*, the baddie, Oddjob, throws a razor-edged bowler hat at his enemies as a weapon. The original prop was later sold at auction for $83,600 (£62,000).

THE COKE CELEBRATED ITS 150TH ANNIVERSARY IN 1999

CELEBRITY CUSTOMERS WERE ASKED TO CUSTOMIZE THEIR OWN HATS

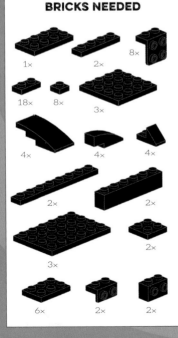

BRICKS NEEDED

1×   2×   8×

18×   8×   3×

4×   4×   4×

2×   2×

3×   2×

6×   2×   2×

YOU CAN MAKE IT

Make a bowler hat fit for a prime minister with these easy instructions.

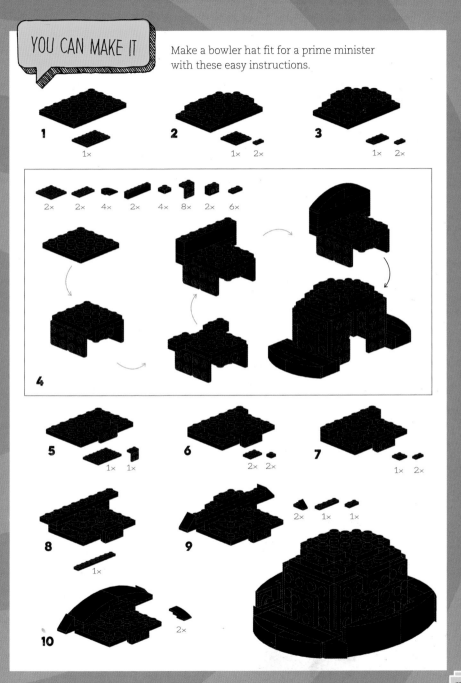

OXO TOWER

This prime spot on London's South Bank housed a power station until it was bought by the company that made OXO stock cubes—the Liebig Extract of Meat Company. They wanted to put their name up in lights. Banned from putting up an advert, they built the windows of the tower in shapes that just so happened to resemble an O, an X, and another O.

Everybody still calls it the OXO Tower, but OXO Tower Wharf (oxotower.co.uk) is now owned and managed by a local social enterprise, the Coin Street Community Builders, and houses co-operative flats, design studios, shops, galleries, restaurants, and cafés.

FOWL PLAY

In December 1945 six men staged an armed robbery at the OXO Tower, stealing more than 100 turkeys!

Channeling "warehouse chic"

The tower is lit red at night

ALL THE PIES

In the 1970s the building was used for producing "long eggs" (elongated hardboiled eggs) to be inserted in the middle of meat pies!

EXCLUSIVE EATS

The exclusive Oxo Tower Brasserie is on the building's 8th floor, with priceless views of the city. You won't find any OXO cubes on the menu here!

BATTERSEA POWER STATION

Battersea Power Station is one of South London's best-known monuments, its four smokestacks famously celebrated on Pink Floyd's *Animals* album cover. It was designed by the same person who created the city's iconic red telephone box (see page 12). The station was snuffed out in 1983 and left in limbo for more than 30 years, but it's now being redeveloped as seriously fancy flats, shops, and restaurants. There will be two brand new tube stations and the US Embassy is even relocating nearby.

The station's iconic white chimneys have been painstakingly dismantled, restored, and reconstructed brick by brick to make them shiny and new.

The building was designed to look like a cathedral. It is Europe's largest brick building.

10 DOWNING STREET

CITY OF WESTMINSTER

Downing Street is named after the grumpy former diplomat George Downing.

Britain's prime minister (PM) has lived at Number 10 Downing Street since 1735. Here, for nearly three centuries PMs have eaten, drunk, snoozed, and run the country (not necessarily all at once). Recent years have seen some PMs moving to the more spacious apartment at 11 Downing Street.

The glossy black door at Number 10 looks like painted wood but it was actually replaced with bomb-proof metal in 1991. There is a brass doorbell but no one rings it as the door is watched via security cameras 24/7. PMs are never even given the keys to their home! Armed guards let them in and out instead.

IMAGINE THE STORIES WE KITTIES COULD TELL!

PALMERSTON

CHIEF MOUSER

Number 10 is one of the most heavily guarded buildings in Britain, and it's even protected from mice. It has its own cat—Larry—with the official title Chief Mouser (CM). He can often be found fighting with his black-and-white rival, Palmerston, who is CM at the Foreign and Commonwealth Office. Both were originally rescue cats.

MELLOW YELLOW

10 Downing St is painted black but the bricks are actually yellow underneath. The city's smog made the originals so dirty that they had to be painted during the 1960s.

LARRY

TURN OVER TO MAKE

NUMBER 10

Make your own mini replica of the most famous door in the world. It's not bomb-proof but it looks good enough for a PM.

BRICKS NEEDED

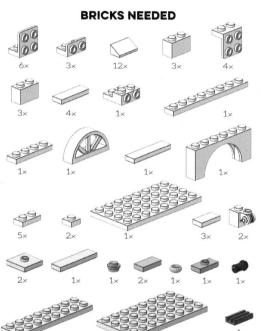

6× 3× 12× 3× 4×

3× 4× 1× 1×

1× 1× 1× 1×

5× 2× 1× 3× 2×

2× 1× 1× 2× 1× 1× 1×

1× 1× 4×

1× 2× 5× 1× 2×

2× 1× 2× 1× 2× 1× 3× 1×

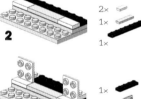

1 1× 1×

2 2× 1× 1×

3 1× 2×

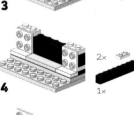

4 2× 1×

5 1× 2× 2× 2×

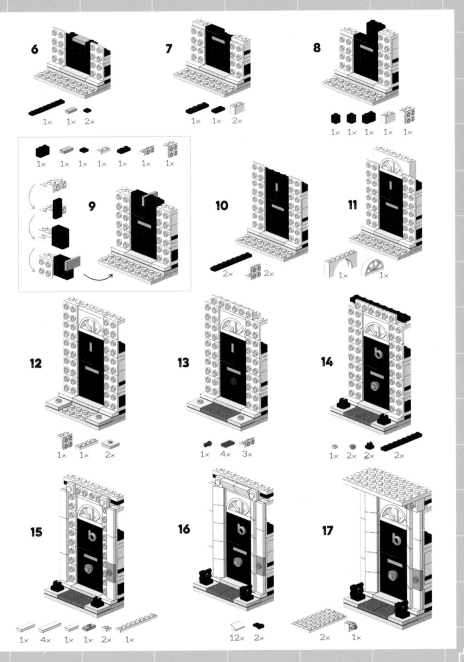

6   1× 1× 2×

7   1× 1× 2×

8   1× 1× 1× 1× 1×

9   1× 1× 1× 1× 1× 1× 1×

10   2× 2×

11   1× 1×

12   1× 1× 2×

13   1× 4× 3×

14   1× 2× 2× 2×

15   1× 4× 1× 1× 2× 1×

16   12× 2×

17   2× 1×

Houses of Parliament

The Houses of Parliament is the heart of UK politics. Officially called the Palace of Westminster, the oldest part is the medieval Westminster Hall. More than 900 years old, it is one of only a few bits that survived a raging fire in 1834. That was particularly lucky as the amazing 1394 roof was the first of its kind. Despite being made of huge, heavy wooden beams, it isn't held up by a single column!

CONSTITUTIONALLY, THE QUEEN IS NOT ALLOWED TO ENTER THE HOUSE OF COMMONS.

WESTMINSTER BRIDGE IS PAINTED THE SAME GREEN AS THE BENCHES.

Westminster Hall's unique roof

"Frontbenchers" sit and debate here

Two sides of the house

Parliament is split into two "houses" who sit in different rooms. The green House of Commons is the lower house, where elected Members of Parliament (MPs) sit. The members of the red-decorated House of Lords traditionally inherited their titles, but nowadays it also has peers selected in other ways. Both houses debate and vote on laws, which are then presented to the Queen. At the annual State Opening of Parliament in May, the Queen takes her throne in the House of Lords, having arrived in her gold-trimmed Irish State Coach from Buckingham Palace (her crown travels alone in its very own coach.) Bling, much?!

THE BIG GUY

You'll recognize the Elizabeth Tower. That's the real name for Big Ben, the world-famous clock tower at the Houses of Parliament. Big Ben is actually the biggest bell inside, which first chimed in 1859. It weighs as much as a small elephant, and when it was first made it needed 16 horses to haul it through London to the tower. Londoners soon nicknamed it, but no one is quite sure why.

Big Ben is accurate to the second

BIG BEN IN NUMBERS

9 foot- (2.7m-) long hour-hand

14 foot- (4.2m-) long minute-hand

23 foot- (7m-) wide dials

2 foot- (60cm-) high numbers

Tower of London

The Tower of London has a dark past. Its 1,000 years of history echo with the crimes and punishments of monarchs, traitors, and torturers. It is a formidable royal fortress, medieval palace, and priceless treasure house.

Off with their heads

There was once a time when anyone important who upset a monarch risked having their head cut off here, on Tower Green. Most prisoners had their heads lopped off in front of a baying crowd on Tower Hill, but this five-star spot was reserved for the most important aristocratic prisoners. Three English queens were beheaded here: Anne Boleyn (1536), Catherine Howard (1542), and Lady Jane Grey (1554). There is now a glass cushion memorial in the exact spot.

BEEFY SECURITY

Forty Yeoman Warders guard the Tower of London. They live with their families in the Tower and are nicknamed "Beefeaters" because they were originally paid with meat instead of money. Their job is a ceremonial one even though they are all ex-soldiers. One Beefeater has the title of "Ravenmaster" as he looks after the ravens.

A Beefeater in uniform

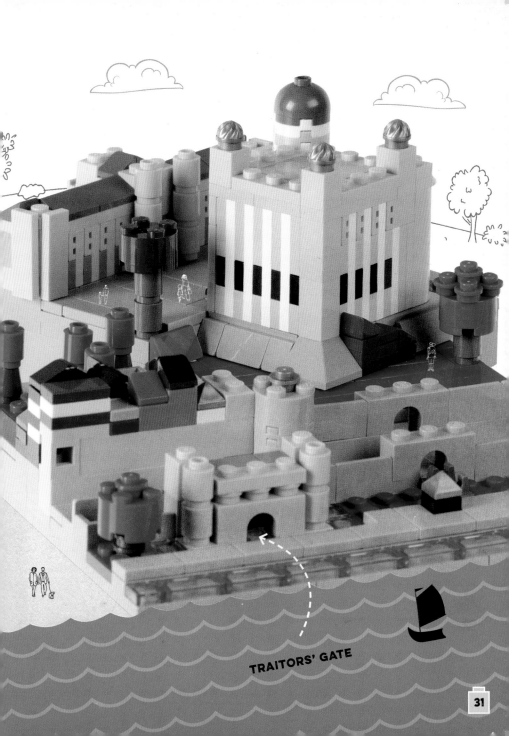

TRAITORS' GATE

Crown Jewels

The Tower of London's Waterloo Barracks is the home of the crown jewels, which are in a very real sense priceless. The royal family's most precious jewels are kept under strict lock and key. The British crown jewels include ten—yes, ten—crowns! There are also swords, orbs, scepters, and other bling things needed to crown British monarchs. The whole super-shiny collection is kept behind extra-thick glass and protected by the hi-tech security. That's because it's worth $5–8 billion (£3–5 billion)!

Imperial Crown of India, worn by George V

The tower also has an extensive armory

IMPERIAL BLING

The Imperial State Crown is set with 2,868 diamonds, including the 317-carat Second Star of Africa (Cullinan II). The oldest stone is probably the St. Edward's Sapphire. It's said to be from a ring worn by Edward the Confessor, the king nearly 1,000 years ago. Edward's grave was opened and it was taken from his finger. The crown is worn by the Queen at the State Opening of Parliament (see p.28).

THE BIG ONE

The State Scepter with Cross is topped with the largest colorless diamond in the world—the First Star of Africa (or Cullinan I). It was cut from the biggest diamond ever found, which was more than 4 inches (10cm) long. Discovered in a South African mine, one of the managers poked it out of a tunnel wall with his stick.

STOP THIEF!

In 1671, Thomas Blood and his gang tried to steal the crown jewels and nearly got away with it. Blood tricked the keeper of the jewels into letting him see them. Then he knocked the keeper out, flattened Edward's crown with a mallet and hid it under his cloak. He even stuffed an orb down his breeches!

TURN OVER TO MAKE

Orb

The queen's orb features amethyst, diamonds, rubies, pearls, sapphires, and emeralds. This model is a bit less expensive to build...!

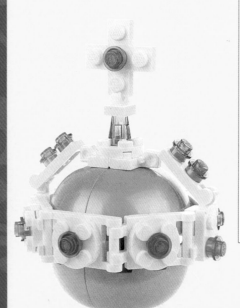

BRICKS NEEDED

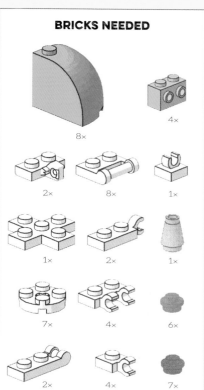

8×

4×

2×   8×   1×

1×   2×   1×

7×   4×   6×

2×   4×   7×

1

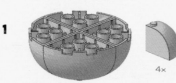

4×

2

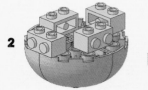

4×

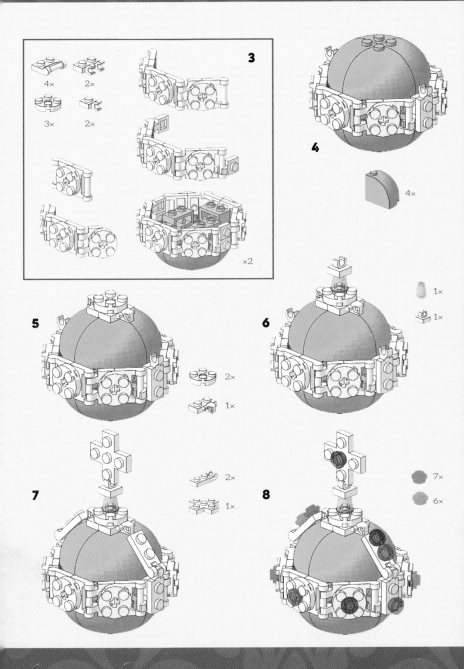

3

4×   2×

3×   2×

×2

4

4×

5

2×

1×

6

1×

1×

7

2×

1×

8

7×

6×

Raven

Ravens have lived at the Tower of London for centuries. Legend has it that if they ever leave, the kingdom will fall, so there are always at least six of them kept at the Tower by royal decree.

The birds have one wing clipped to stop them flying off but they are spoilt rotten, with daily raw meat and blood-soaked biscuits. In spite of this, birds do sometimes decide to leave, or behave so badly they have to go. One raven flew off and was last spotted outside a London pub!

YOU CAN MAKE IT!

Scientists have discovered that ravens are as intelligent as apes. This model raven certainly has a clever glint in its eye.

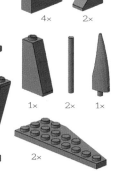

BRICKS NEEDED

1×   7×   5×   1×   2×   2×   2×   4×   2×

1×   2×   2×   5×   2×   4×   9×

5×   4×   1×   10×   1×   2×   3×   1×   2×   1×

2×   2×

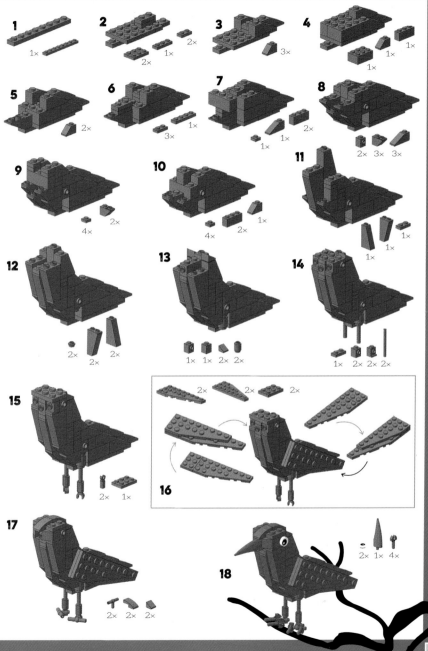

STOCKS

Life at the Tower of London was hardly a bundle of laughs. King Henry I was the first monarch to use the Royal residence as a state prison in 1100, but it was during the Tudor era in the 16th and 17th centuries that things really got nasty. Prisoners were tied on a rack and stretched, or hung by their wrists from the ceiling in manacles, to make them confess their crimes.

Royal prisoners

Hardcore criminals were not the only "guests"—several members of the royal family were incarcerated here, too. In the 15th century, the two young sons of King Edward IV were locked up there by their uncle Richard so that he could take over the throne. In 1536 King Henry VIII had his second wife, Anne Boleyn, tried and executed here—clearing the way for him to marry someone new.

BLOODY RIVERBANKS

William the Conqueror cleverly had the Tower of London built on the banks of the River Thames—London's lifeline to and from the outside world. Prisoners sent to the Tower would arrive by boat along the river, entering through Traitors' Gate. Today, the once bloody riverbanks buzz with fun as Londoners enjoy their waterfront playground.

Horrid Henry!

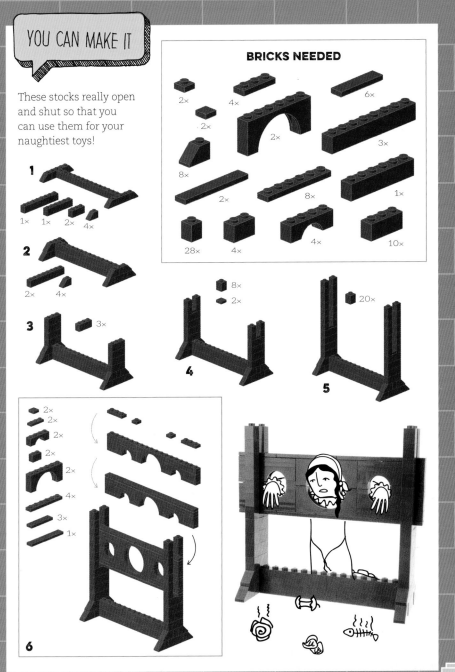

YOU CAN MAKE IT

These stocks really open and shut so that you can use them for your naughtiest toys!

BRICKS NEEDED

UNION JACK

The Union Jack has been the UK's national flag since 1908. It combines England's red St. George's cross, Scotland's white St. Andrew's saltire, and the red saltire of St. Patrick to represent the island of Ireland.

When the Queen is in residence at Buckingham Place the square yellow, red, and blue Royal Standard is flown; if she's not in residence, it's the Union Jack.

ZIG-A-ZIG-AH!

Geri Halliwell, aka Ginger Spice, made pop history when she performed with the Spice Girls at the 1997 BRIT Awards. She made her "Cool Britannia" minidress by stitching a humble tea towel onto the front of a black Gucci dress. Later it was sold at auction for $56,856 (£41,300). When the Spice Girls reunited for a tour in 2007 she wore a replica covered in crystals.

Flags flying for the Queen's jubilee

UK government buildings are required to fly the Union Jack at full-mast an average of 23 times a year.

Westminster Abbey

It doesn't get more royal than this. Westminster Abbey serves up the country's history on cold slabs of stone. It has been the site of the coronation of every British monarch since William the Conqueror was crowned in 1066, with the exception of a couple of unlucky Eds who were either murdered (Edward V) or retired (Edward VIII) before the magic moment.

PRINCE WILLIAM MARRIED KATE MIDDLETON HERE IN 2011.

MADE FOR MONKS

When the Abbey was first built nearly 1,000 years ago it was on an island. Over time, the land has been drained so it's not on an island any more. For centuries monks lived here and the Abbey had its own farm and gardens. There's still a peaceful herb garden, where the monks once grew the plants they needed for food and to make medicine.

ST. EDWARD WAS THE FOUNDER OF THE ABBEY.

THE MOST SACRED SPOT IN THE ABBEY IS THE SHRINE OF ST. EDWARD THE CONFESSOR.

Christmas Day chaos

William the Conqueror, crowned at the Abbey on Christmas Day, 1066, had a coronation to remember. He came from Normandy in Northern France and had invaded England, forcing London to accept him as ruler. At the ceremony, the English nobles were asked to accept him as king and they shouted their agreement—which is traditional. But the French guards outside didn't know that. They thought there was trouble and started setting fire to buildings!

ST. EDWARD'S REMAINS ARE THE ONLY COMPLETE SAINT'S BODY IN BRITAIN. OTHERS HAVE BEEN SPLIT APART TO BE USED AS HOLY RELICS.

YUCK!

THE END IS NIGH

In front of the Abbey's altar a marble pavement from 1268 predicts the end of the world in AD 19,693, so we have a little way to go still!

The Abbey's grand north entrance

THE ORIGINAL BUILDING WAS DECLARED HOLY JUST A FEW WEEKS BEFORE ST. EDWARD'S DEATH.

ROYAL RESTING PLACE

Among the 450 tombs and monuments are 17 monarch's graves, including those of Tudor rulers Henry VIII, Mary and Elizabeth I. It's also the final resting place of many notable non-royals, including scientists Charles Darwin and Sir Isaac Newton, authors Geoffrey Chaucer and Charles Dickens, and many other greats (William Shakespeare, Jane Austen, Charlotte Brontë).

Coronation Chair

The wooden Coronation Chair at Westminster Abbey was made on the orders of Edward I in 1300. He had a space put underneath to house the Stone of Scone—the sacred stone of Scotland that Scottish kings sit on when they get crowned. Now the stone is in Edinburgh Castle but it will be brought back for future coronations. Every monarch since the early 14th century has been crowned on this chair (apart from joint-monarchs Mary II and William III, who had their own chairs fashioned for the event).

SPLINTERED BUT SURVIVED

In 1914, suffragettes fighting for women's votes put a small bomb underneath, which blew a piece off. Then in 1950, Scottish students stole the Stone of Scone from under it, damaging the chair and accidentally dropping the stone and breaking it in half.

SCHOOLBOY GRAFFITI

The Coronation Chair had lots of graffiti carved on it by Westminster schoolboys in the 1700s and 1800s.

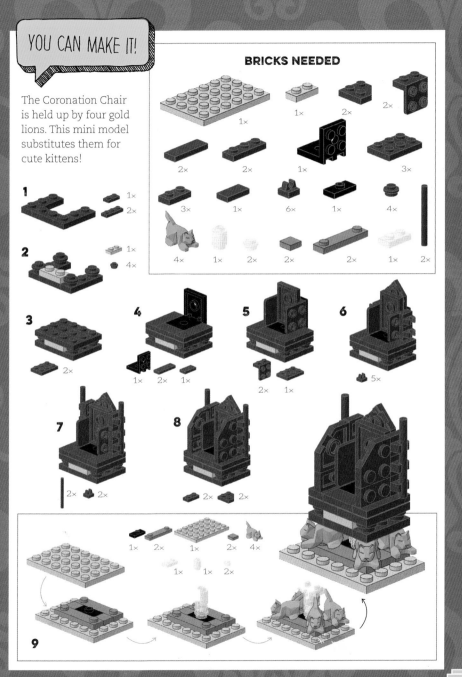

YOU CAN MAKE IT!

The Coronation Chair is held up by four gold lions. This mini model substitutes them for cute kittens!

BRICKS NEEDED

1× 1× 2× 2×

2× 2× 1× 3×

3× 1× 6× 1× 4×

4× 1× 2× 2× 2× 1× 2×

1 1× 2×

2 1× 4×

3 2×

4 1× 2× 1×

5 2× 1×

6 5×

7 2× 2×

8 2× 2×

9 1× 2× 1× 2× 4×

1× 1× 2×

TRAFALGAR SQUARE

"The Invisible Enemy Should Not Exist"

Trafalgar Square is the true center of London, where thousands of revellers see in the New Year, and locals congregate for open-air cinema, Christmas celebrations and political protests. It is dominated by the 170 foot- (52m-) high Nelson's Column, which honours Admiral Lord Horatio Nelson, who led his fleet's heroic victory over Napoleon in 1805. It is ringed by four large bronze lions.

The Fourth Plinth

Three of the square's four plinths are occupied by nobles. The fourth plinth remained empty for more than 150 years until the Royal Society of Arts used it to create the Fourth Plinth Commission, "the smallest sculpture park in the world." Changing artworks include a clear resin copy of the plinth turned upside down, a giant thumbs-up, a bright blue cockerel and a winged bull made from tin cans, see above.

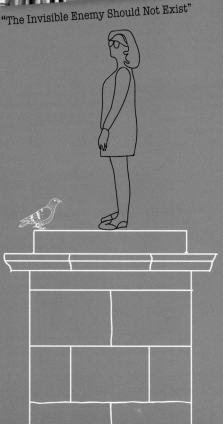

THE WORLD'S
SMALLEST
SCULPTURE
PARK

49

Bronze won in battle

The bronze used to make the lions came from cannons captured from the Battle of Trafalgar—Nelson's greatest victory. His forces beat Napoleon in a sea battle but he paid with his life when he was shot on deck by a French sniper. His statue stands on top of the column, minus an eye and an arm, both which he lost while fighting.

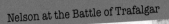

Nelson at the Battle of Trafalgar

Nelson's column in Trafalgar Square

CAT PAWS

Victorian artist Sir Edwin Landseer was commissioned to design the lions but it took him nine years to create them. He visited London Zoo to watch the lions there and asked if he could have a dead one. It took years for a lion to die but eventually he got one. He started to make models of it, but the body began to rot before he could finish, which is why the lions have pet cat paws.

THE LIONS IN NUMBERS

11 feet (3.4m) high
20 feet (6.1m) long
27 parts are riveted together per lion

51

CITY OF LONDON
DRAGON

The City of London's official symbol is the dragon—and that's why there are so many of these magical beasts infesting the capital! The boundaries marking the edges of the city are guarded by silver dragons standing on plinths,with upswept wings and pointed tongues, holding shields and swords. The original inspiration was the two 7 foot- (2.1m-) high dragons on Victoria Embankment.

BEASTS OF THE BOROUGH

Each London borough has its own coat-of-arms and many of them show mythical (and real) beasts, including lions, griffins, dragons, stags, boars, and bulls.

GGGGRRR!

SCALY SLEEPOVERS

London's Natural History Museum is home to reconstructed skeletons of the original mega-monsters—dinosaurs! Life-size animatronic dinos roar at visitors as they walk past, including a terrifying moving T. rex that senses passers-by and bares its teeth! The bravest enthusiasts can book in for a sleepover at the museum or a torch-lit tour of the dino gallery.

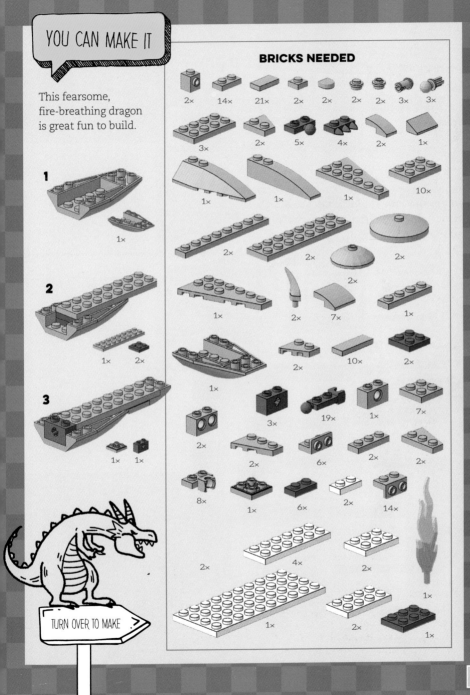

YOU CAN MAKE IT

This fearsome, fire-breathing dragon is great fun to build.

BRICKS NEEDED

2× 14× 21× 2× 2× 2× 2× 3× 3×

3× 2× 5× 4× 2× 1×

1× 1× 1× 10×

2× 2× 2× 2×

1× 2× 7× 1×

2× 10× 2×

3× 19× 1× 7×

2× 2× 6× 2× 2×

8× 1× 6× 2× 14×

2× 4× 2×

1× 2× 1×

1×

1

1×

2

1× 2×

3

1× 1×

TURN OVER TO MAKE

4

1× 1×
1× 4×

5

1× 1×

6

1× 2× 1×

7

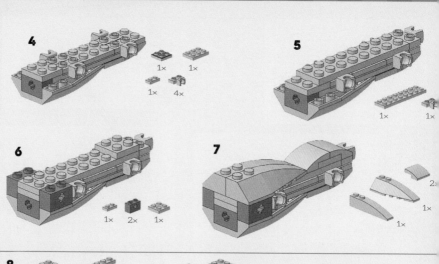

2×
1×
1×

8

1× 1× 1× 1× 2× 1×
1× 1× 1×

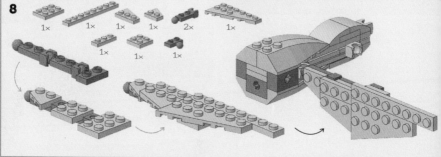

9

1× 1× 1× 2× 1× 1× 1× 1× 1×

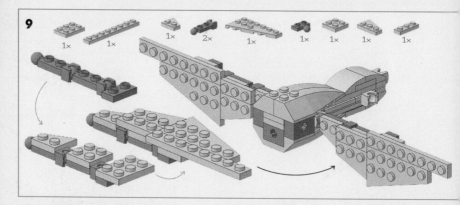

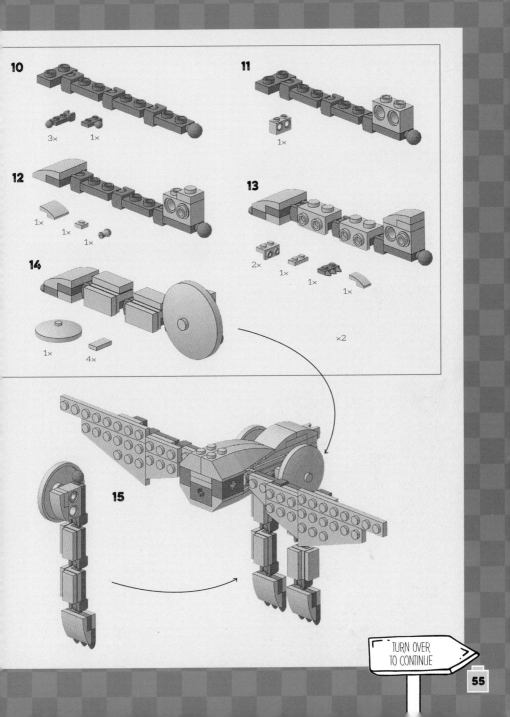

10

3× 1×

11

1×

12

1× 1× 1×

13

2× 1× 1× 1× ×2

14

1× 4×

15

TURN OVER TO CONTINUE

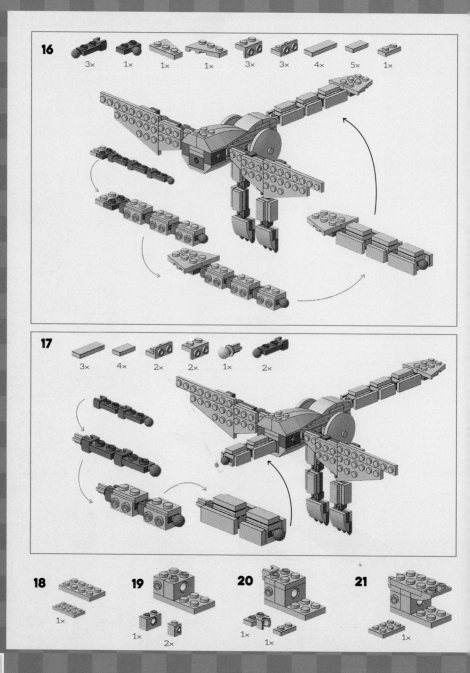

16
3× 1× 1× 1× 3× 3× 4× 5× 1×

17
3× 4× 2× 2× 1× 2×

18
1×

19
1× 2×

20
1× 1×

21
1×

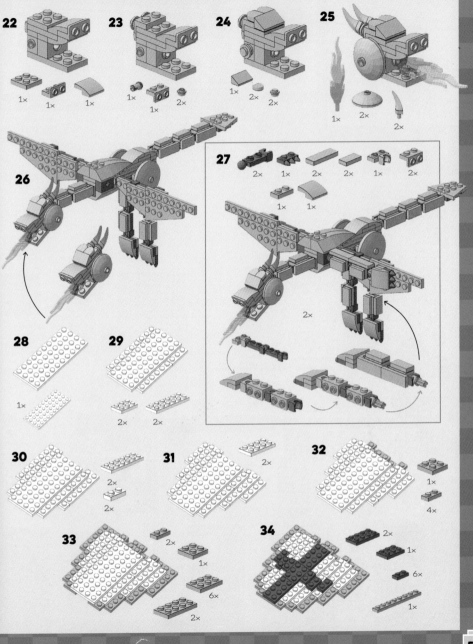

22 1× 1× 1×

23 1× 1× 2×

24 1× 2× 2×

25 1× 2× 2×

26

27 2× 1× 2× 1× 2×
1× 1×
2×

28 1×

29 2× 2×

30 2× 2×

31 2×

32 1× 4×

33 2× 1× 6× 2×

34 2× 1× 6× 1×

The London Eye

The London Eye is the world's biggest rotating observation wheel, 443 feet (135m) tall and 394 feet (120m) wide. On a clear day the views stretch 25 miles (40km)—that's about as far as Windsor Castle so remember to wave at the Queen. More than 3.5 million people cram into its 32 capsules every year. That's more than visit the Egyptian pyramids or India's Taj Mahal!

The Eye overlooks the River Thames. England's longest river runs right through the city and it was probably the reason why people settled here in the first place, around 750,000 years ago when it was a marshy wilderness. The first Londoners built their prehistoric huts where they could fish and get across the river. They built wooden walkways over the marshes, too. The remains of one walkway were discovered in Greenwich, dating back 6,000 years. That's more than 500 years older than Stonehenge!

MUDDY LARKS

Muddying your hands might sound like a laugh but imagine having to do it to stay alive. "Mudlarks" were poor Victorian children who scrabbled on the river's banks looking for things to sell. They savenged wood, tin or, if they were lucky, a lost brooch.

CLEOPATRA'S NEEDLE

No single monument captures the English love of history and eccentricity quite like Cleopatra's Needle. The Egyptian obelisk was transported to London in 1877 and planted on the Victoria Embankment a year later. A time capsule was hidden in its base. Its said to include a portrait of Queen Victoria, a railway guide, hairpins, the *Bible*, toys, a baby's bottle, and pictures of English beauties of the day.

Sphinxes guard the needle's base

Large parts of London are below the high-water mark of the River Thames. The Embankment was built between 1864 and 1870 and is an amazing feat of engineering that channels the water between its huge walls. It stops large areas of the city from being flooded. It also provides places for boats to dock and for pedestrians to walk.

A CURIOUS CURSE?

The needle is around 3,460 years old and comes from an ancient city called Heliopolis. The hieroglyphs all over it commemorate Ancient Egyptian battle victories and are actually nothing to do with Cleopatra. It was given to Britain in the 1800s by the ruler of Egypt and was sailed over to the UK. During the voyage a storm killed six crewmen and the needle was nearly lost for good, leading people to say it was cursed.

Queen's Guards

The Queen of England lives at Buckingham Palace. The grand white building is used to host state visits, royal ceremonies and Her Majesty's famous garden parties. Queen Elizabeth II divides her time between here, Windsor Castle, and Balmoral castle in Scotland.

The Queen's Guards stand on duty at Buckingham Palace and St. James's Palace. They sport red tunics and bearskin hats in summer and greatcoats in winter. Their uniforms come from a time when soldiers fought on foot. The tall bearskin caps were devised to make them look taller in battle and their red tunics made it harder for the enemy to count them on the battlefield (they tend to blur into each other in a crowd).

BUCKINGHAM PALACE IN NUMBERS

78 bathrooms

350 clocks

775 rooms

EAT LIKE A ROYAL

Buckingham Palace is also the venue for royal banquets. It takes three days to lay the enormous table with thousands of pieces of cutlery, glasses and napkins. Each guest gets a space of 16½ inches (42cm) for their setting, and it's all carefully measured. During the mega-dinners there are so many courses that staff use a traffic-light system behind the scenes.

THE WORLD'S MOST EXPENSIVE HOME

The London home of the queen is officially the world's most expensive, worth over $1.4 billion (£1 billion). Its Throne Room boasts two pink velvet chairs with golden sphinx-shaped armrests and his-and-hers monograms. For Prince William's wedding it became a "chillax" room, complete with DJ.

TURN OVER TO MAKE

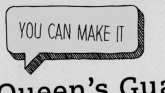

Queen's Guards

The guards at Buckingham Palace are strictly forbidden from smiling. This model is similarly stony-faced.

BRICKS NEEDED

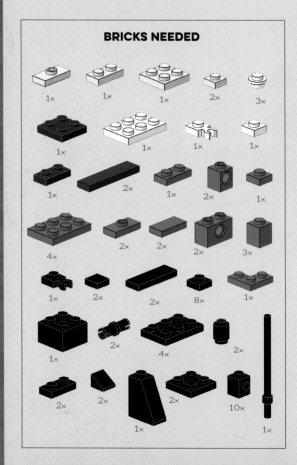

1× 1× 1× 2× 3×

1× 1× 1× 1×

1× 2× 1× 2× 1×

4× 2× 2× 2× 3×

1× 2× 2× 8× 1×

2× 4× 2×

1× 1×

2× 2× 2× 10× 1×

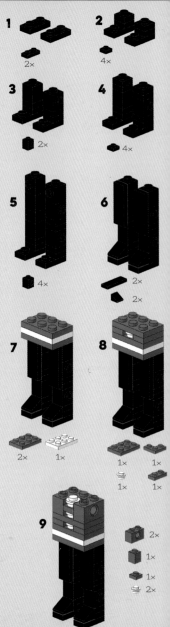

1   2×
2   4×
3   2×
4   4×
5   4×
6   2× 2×
7   2× 1×
8   1× 1× 1× 1×
9   2× 1× 1× 2×

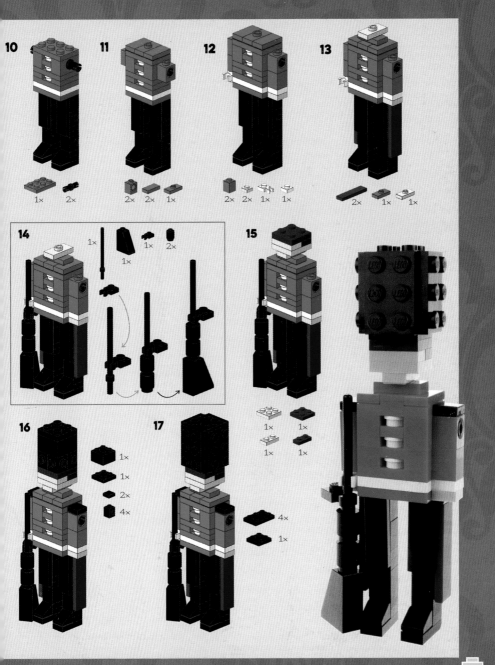

ST. PAUL'S CATHEDRAL

THE BIGGEST BELLS ARE GREAT PAUL, WEIGHING MORE THAN A MALE ELEPHANT, AND GREAT TOM, WEIGHING AS MUCH AS A FEMALE ELEPHANT.

Royal events aplenty have taken place at St. Paul's Cathedral, including luxurious weddings. It was designed by Sir Christopher Wren, who wanted to make a dome that was grand on the outside but not too echoey and large on the inside. The solution was to build it in three layers, like the inside of an onion. This unique structure made the cathedral Wren's masterpiece.

ST. PAUL'S BOASTS 12 BELLS AND ONE OF THE LOUDEST PEALS IN THE WORLD.

View from the Whispering Gallery

GREAT
TOM

GREAT TOM TOLLS
OUT THE BAD
NEWS IF A MEMBER
OF THE ROYAL
FAMILY DIES.

BT Tower

Owned by phone company BT, the BT Tower was the city's tallest structure when it opened in 1966 and visible from almost everywhere in central London. Strangely, the tower was an official "secret" and didn't appear on maps until 1993, when Member of Parliament Kate Hoey used her parliamentary privilege to "confirm" its existence!

The tower is still a major communications hub and doubles up as an air-pollution monitor. It is also a listed building, which means getting special permission to change it.

50TH BIRTHDAY

To mark the tower's 50th anniversary, its revolving restaurant reopened its doors for two weeks only. The Top of the Tower restaurant was an icon. In the 1960s Muhammad Ali, Tom Jones and The Beatles were among the 4,000 daily visitors.

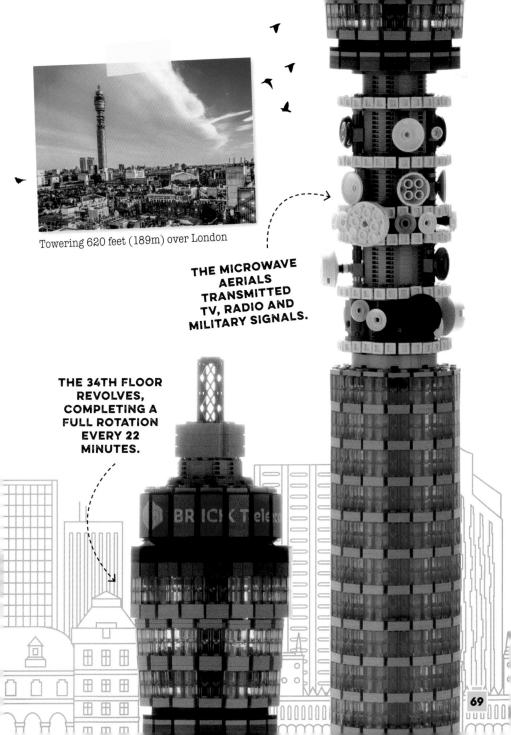

Towering 620 feet (189m) over London

THE MICROWAVE AERIALS TRANSMITTED TV, RADIO AND MILITARY SIGNALS.

THE 34TH FLOOR REVOLVES, COMPLETING A FULL ROTATION EVERY 22 MINUTES.

BR ICK Tele

THE BRITISH MUSEUM

The country's largest museum and one of the oldest and finest in the world, this famous museum is home to Egyptian, Etruscan, Greek, Roman, European, and Middle Eastern treasures, among others. Inside, the Great Court has an amazing glass-and-steel latticed roof. At its center is the Reading Room—Mahatma Gandhi was a cardholder.

Some of the most interesting artefacts here are: the Rosetta Stone, the key to deciphering Egyptian hieroglyphics; the controversial Parthenon Sculptures, taken from Athens by Lord Elgin; the collection of Egyptian mummies.

BURIED TREASURE

460 years ago someone was on the run and had to bury a fortune fast! That's thought to be the story behind the Fishpool Hoard—1,237 gold coins (plus jewelery) now on display. It was a time of rebellion and the person who buried the stash could have been on the losing side of a battle.

The Great Court and latticed roof

The Fishpool
Hoard was worth
$459,570
(£300,000) when
it was buried.

TURN OVER TO MAKE

THE BRITISH MUSEUM

The museum entrance has sculptures that show the human race being educated by its artifacts. This model will certainly give you a fun lesson in LEGO® building!

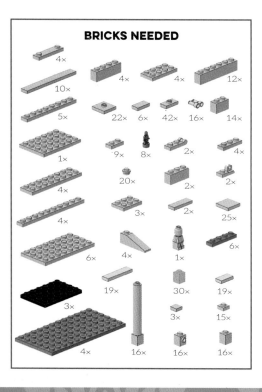

BRICKS NEEDED

4×
4×
4×
12×
10×
5×
22×
6×
42×
16×
14×
1×
9×
8×
2×
4×
4×
20×
2×
2×
3×
2×
25×
6×
4×
1×
6×
19×
30×
19×
3×
3×
15×
4×
16×
16×
16×

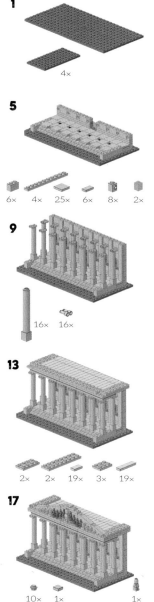

1

4×

5

6×
4×
25×
6×
8×
2×

9

16×
16×

13

2×
2×
19×
3×
19×

17

10×
1×
1×
4×

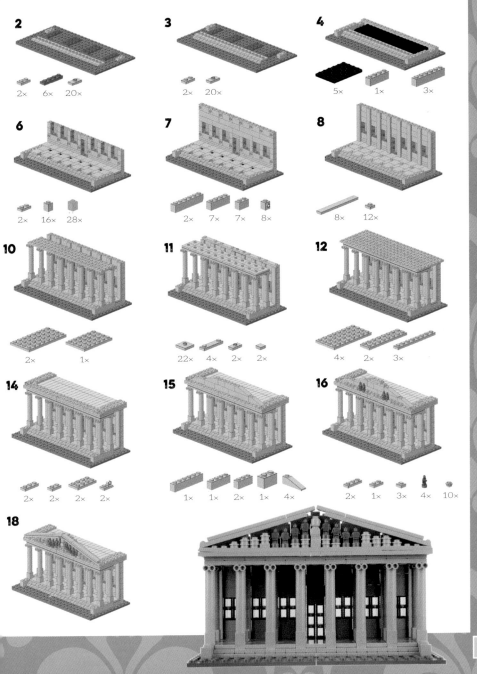

2
2× 6× 20×

3
2× 20×

4
5× 1× 3×

6
2× 16× 28×

7
2× 7× 7× 8×

8
8× 12×

10
2× 1×

11
22× 4× 2× 2×

12
4× 2× 3×

14
2× 2× 2× 2×

15
1× 1× 2× 1× 4×

16
2× 1× 3× 4× 10×

18

The Shard

Only Londoners can dine in a glass Shard, work inside a Cheese Grater, shop in a Stealth Bomber and negotiate business deals in a Gherkin. These are the names of some of 21st-century-London's newest buildings. The Walkie Talkie is a skyscraper shaped like a hand-held radio. This feat of engineering quickly earned the nickname "Walkie Scorchie" after cars parked beneath its reflective exterior started melting in the sun!

There are a total of 82 floors in the skyscraper

FEARLESS FOX

When The Shard was being built a wild fox managed to get in and climb up to the 72nd floor, where he lived eating food scraps left lying around by the builders. When he was discovered staff nicknamed him Romeo. He was rescued, checked by vets and then set free, back to his life roaming the streets.

The Shard is the highest skyscraper in Western Europe (1,017 feet/310m). It has 95 storeys, which pack in award-winning restaurants, a five-star hotel, offices and London's highest viewing gallery. The architect, Renzo Piano, wanted the building to look like an iceberg rising from the river nearby.

LONDON MONUMENT

In 1666, the Great Fire of London started in a bakery in Pudding Lane and soon swept through the whole city, destroying thousands of homes. Much of the medieval city was destroyed, with 13,200 houses reduced to rubble and an estimated 70,000 people made homeless (though only a half-dozen died).

The fire is commemorated by the Monument—the world's tallest individual stone column, designed by Sir Christopher Wren. Its height is the exact distance from the column to the place where the fire began, and the gleaming golden urn on top symbolizes flames.

Urn on the monument's top

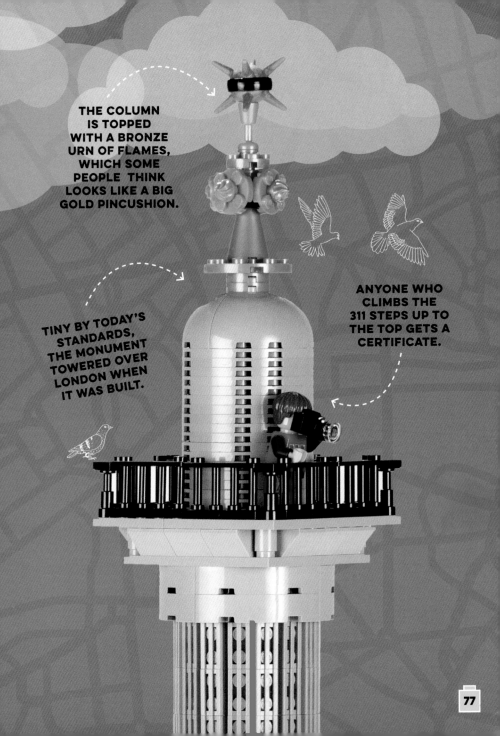

THE COLUMN IS TOPPED WITH A BRONZE URN OF FLAMES, WHICH SOME PEOPLE THINK LOOKS LIKE A BIG GOLD PINCUSHION.

TINY BY TODAY'S STANDARDS, THE MONUMENT TOWERED OVER LONDON WHEN IT WAS BUILT.

ANYONE WHO CLIMBS THE 311 STEPS UP TO THE TOP GETS A CERTIFICATE.

Fish and Chips

Nothing else says "England" quite like the smell of frying fish! Fish and chips often tops the list of the nation's favorite food (occasionally falling behind chicken tikka masala). It's traditionally served wrapped in old newspaper and sprinkled generously with salt and malt vinegar. It's usually made with Atlantic cod, but "chippies" are starting to fry a wider range of fish to conserve the ocean's stocks. Weird and wonderful side dishes include mushy peas and pickled eggs!

A SLIPPERY MEAL

Jellied eels are London's original fast food. Fished for in the River Thames, the wriggling delicacy was cooked, left to cool and only eaten when the liquid had turned to jelly—slime heaven!

THE FIRST CHIP SHOP IN THE WORLD WAS OPENED IN OLD FORD ROAD, EAST LONDON, IN 1860 BY JOSEPH MALIN.

These models look good enough to eat—complete with chips and mushy peas, or an accompaniment of your choice!

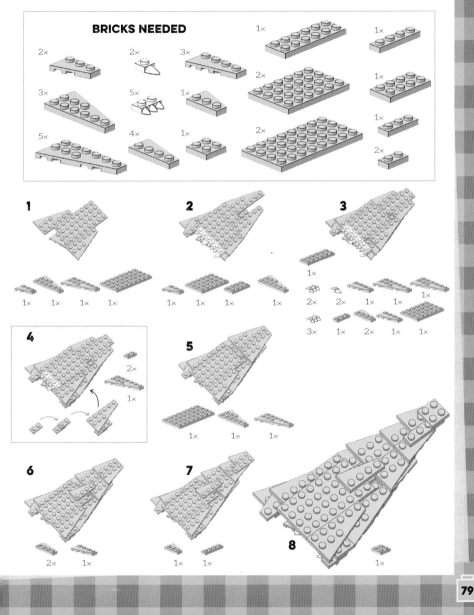

BOROUGH MARKET

Located in the same spot since the 13th century, "London's Larder" has experienced an amazing rebirth in the past 15 years. Borough Market is always overflowing with food lovers, gastronomes, wide-eyed visitors, and Londoners in search of inspiration for their dinner party. The market specializes in upmarket fresh produce. There are plenty of takeaway stands and an almost unreasonable number of cake stalls. Yum!

PRIZED PARMESAN

London diarist Samuel Pepys was caught in the Great Fire of London in 1666 and had to save his most valuable possessions—including a giant wheel of Parmesan cheese! It was too heavy to carry, so he buried it in his garden. Parmesan was very costly in his day. Even today, valuable Parmesans are sometimes stored in bank vaults.

TRAFFIC CHAOS

In the 1700s the market was a much less orderly affair with stalls spilling out all over Borough High Street and causing traffic mayhem. There was an Act of Parliament to close down the market in the streets, which is when it moved to its current location.

Borough Market today

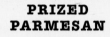

FOOD TRUCK

TOP OF THE TRUCKS

The UK chain MEATliquor started life as a burger van in 2009. Now with 11 restaurants, it made a profit of $22.5 million (£17 million) in 2016.

Food is big business in London. The city's colorful markets and vacant street corners are increasingly occupied by independent food trucks, many of them in repurposed vintage vehicles such as horse boxes, school buses, and even Airstream caravans. On sale are freshly cooked bites from around the globe, from steaming pork buns to bulging burritos, and deep-fried churros dipped in chocolate sauce. Yum!

The KERB collective is the heart of London's street food revolution, attracting the very best food on wheels to sites around the city. Vendors call themselves "KERB-anists." Pistachio-butter doughnuts anyone?

TURN OVER TO MAKE

Make your very easy-to-build food truck. Hipster staff not included!

BRICKS NEEDED

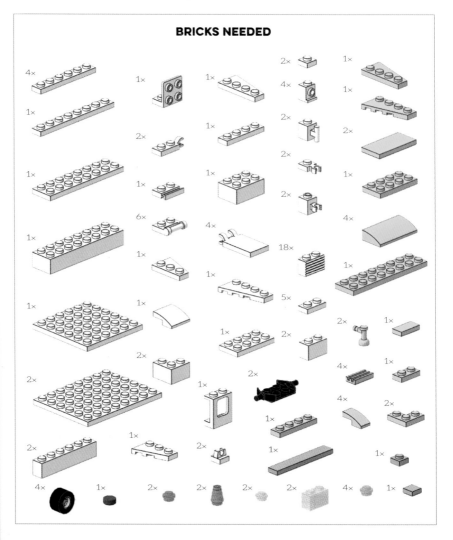

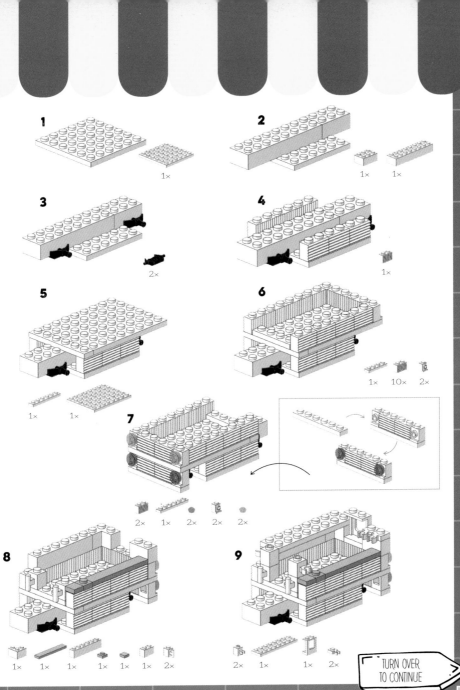

1

2

1×

1× 1×

3

2×

4

1×

5

1× 1×

6

1× 10× 2×

7

2× 1× 2× 2× 2×

8

1× 1× 1× 1× 1× 1× 2×

9

2× 1× 1× 2×

TURN OVER TO CONTINUE

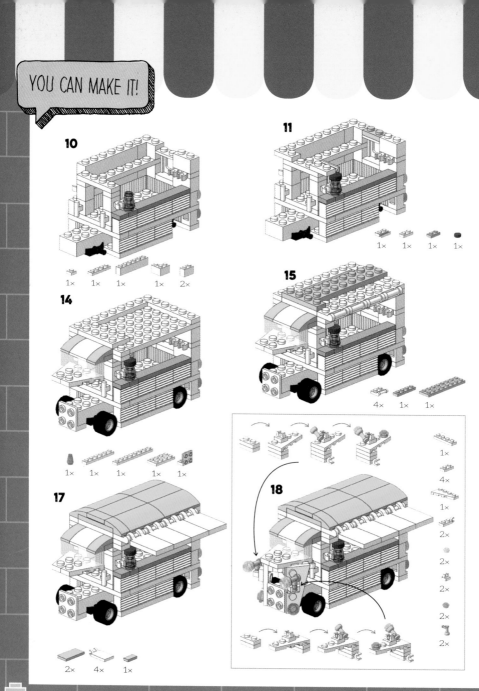

YOU CAN MAKE IT!

10

1× 1× 1× 1× 2×

11

1× 1× 1× 1×

14

1× 1× 1× 1× 1×

15

4× 1× 1×

17

2× 4× 1×

18

1×
4×
1×
2×
2×
2×
2×
2×

12

4×
1×

13

1× 1× 1× 2× 2× 1× 2×

16

2× 4×

19

4× 1× 1×

1× 2×

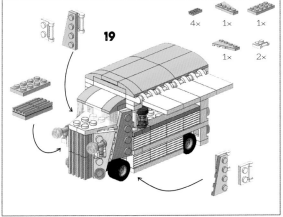

Afternoon Tea

Fortnum & Mason is one of London's poshest grocers. It has sold tea for 300 years, and the tea salon there is a top spot to sip a brew and nibble cucumber sandwiches and jam-slathered scones.

The habit of having afternoon tea and cakes caught on in London in the 1800s. It became a grand party event, with people sending invitations to their friends and wearing their best gloves to eat their cakes and sandwiches.

THE BEES' KNEES

Four beautiful gilded beehives are kept on the roof of Fortnum and Mason. The bees make top quality honey for the shop's customers.

CUPPA ROSIE LEE

Only Londoners born within hearing distance of the bells of St. Mary-Le-Bow Church are true "cockneys." East End cockneys even have their own language.

A "CUPPA ROSIE LEE" IS A NICE CUP OF STRONG ENGLISH TEA (ALWAYS WITH MILK).

THE CORNISH PUT JAM ON THEIR SCONES FIRST, THEN CLOTTED CREAM.

THOSE FROM DEVON SMEAR CREAM ON BOARD FIRST, THEN A BLOB OF JAM.

Chinatown

Chinatown is the hub of the Chinese community in London, and when Chinese New Year comes along people in dragon and lion costumes dance through the streets here.

THEY HAVE STAG HORNS, FISH SCALES AND TIGER PAWS AND ARE SAID TO BRING GOOD LUCK.

CHINESE DRAGONS ARE NOT LIKE SCARY FIRE-BREATHING EUROPEAN DRAGONS.

London's original Chinatown was at Limehouse in the East End of London—even Sherlock Holmes shopped there.

ELEMENTARY MY DEAR...

Although it's just two streets really—this is a lively area with giant Oriental gates, Chinese street signs, pretty red lanterns, restaurants selling steaming noodles, and Asian supermarkets full of curiosities. You can hear lots of different languages and dialects being spoken here, from Cantonese to Mandarin.

THE LONGER THE DRAGON, THE MORE LUCK IT BRINGS.

TURN OVER TO MAKE

Chinese Dragon

This beautiful Chinese dragon is surprisingly
easy to make as a lot of the steps are repeated.

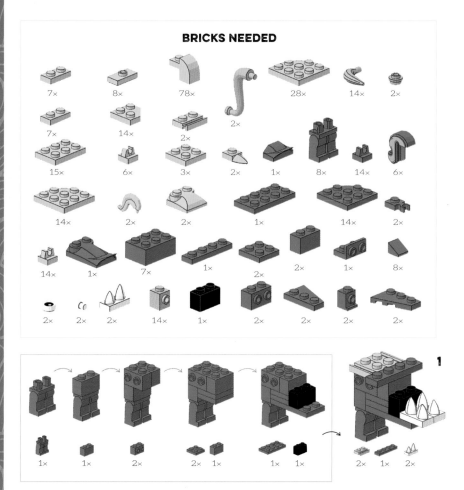

BRICKS NEEDED

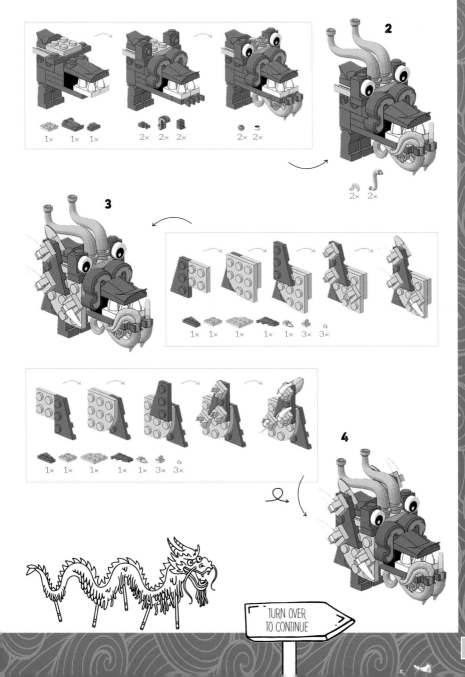

2

3

4

TURN OVER
TO CONTINUE

5

6

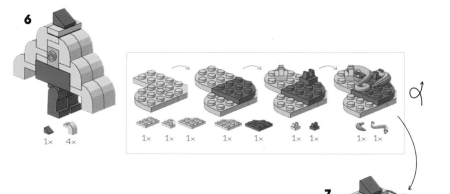

7

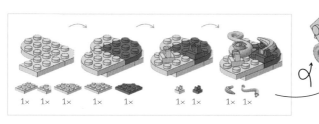

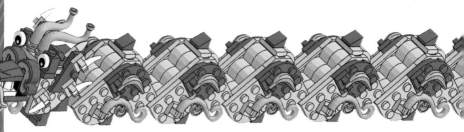

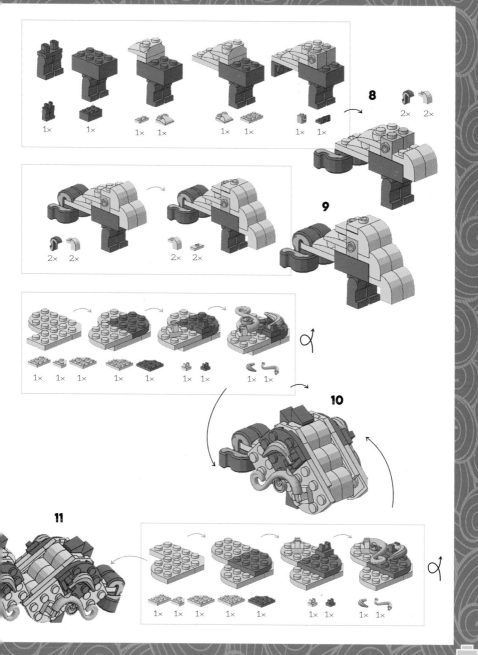

8

2× 2×

9

2× 2×   2× 2×

1× 1×   1× 1×   1× 1×   1× 1×   1× 1×   1× 1×

10

11

1× 1×   1× 1×   1× 1×   1× 1×   1× 1×

Covent Garden

Covent Garden was originally pastureland that belonged to a convent (Covent/convent—get it?), but it has had many different reincarnations. For a long while this elegant piazza hosted a bustling fruit and vegetable market.

London society gathered here in the evenings, looking for some action among the coffee houses, theatres and gambling dens. Crime was common, leading to the formation of a volunteer police force. The market still draws crowds looking for a good time and is full of street performers—from opera singers to human statues and magicians.

Inside the old market

Leicester Square to Covent Garden is London's shortest Tube journey—in fact it only takes 45 seconds!

Covent Garden is home to London's oldest restaurant—Rules on Maiden Lane. It was first opened in 1798 and serves traditional food such as game pie and oysters.

UNDERGROUND TRAIN

The London Underground—or "Tube"—is made up of 11 color-coded lines. Some stations, most famously Embankment and Charing Cross, are much closer in reality than they appear on the map, so you might be better off walking! Author Mark Mason walked the entire length of the London Underground—but overground—for his book *Walk the Lines*.

THE UNDERGROUND IN NUMBERS

1.03 billion passengers per year

250 miles (402km) of track

190 feet (58m) down in the deepest station (Hampstead)

TRAVELING IN STYLE

Sedan chairs were used to get around 18th-century-London. They were carried by two strong men (notorious for their terrible swearing). Inside was enough room to squeeze in the passengers' fancy wigs and gowns.

LONDON TRANSPORT MUSEUM

All aboard for a trip through London's "wheely" interesting history. Visitors get to sit in the cab of a red bus and even drive a Tube train on a Northern Line Underground simulator.

TURN OVER TO MAKE

UNDERGROUND TRAIN

This model sports the Underground's signature go-fast white, blue, and red design. Trains on the Metropolitan Line can run at up to 60 mph (97km/h).

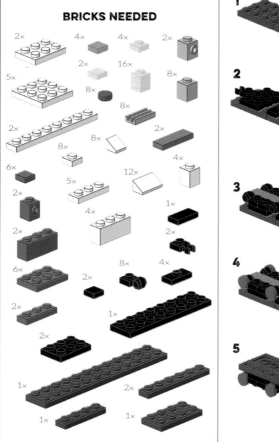

BRICKS NEEDED

2× 4× 4× 2×
2× 16× 8×
5× 8×
8×
2× 8× 2×
8×
6× 4×
5× 12×
2× 1×
4×
2× 2×
6× 8× 4×
2×
2× 1×
2×
1× 2×
1× 1×

1

2
1× 1× 1× 2×

3
4× 1× 2× 2× 2×

4
8× 2×

5
1× 8×

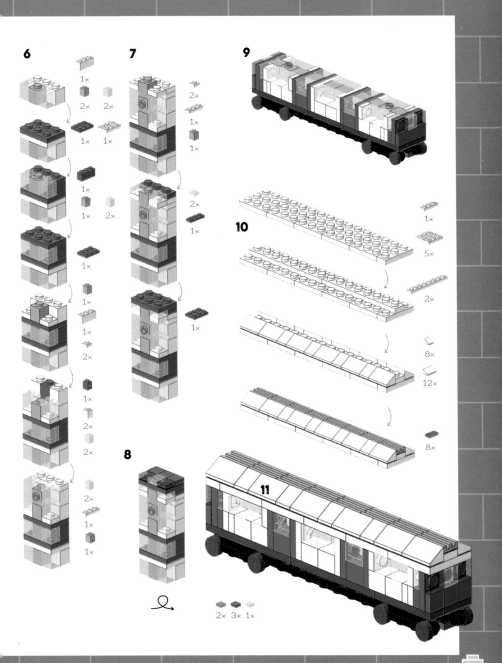

6

1×
2× 2×
1× 1×

1×
1× 2×

1×

1×

1×
2×

1×
2×
2×

2×
1×
1×

7

2×
1×
1×

2×
1×

1×

8

2× 3× 1×

9

10

1×
5×
2×
8×
12×
8×

11

Red Buses

Everyone knows about London's famous red buses. These iconic vehicles zip around the capital at all hours of the day and night, carrying Londoners from A to B.

Six and a half million people use the city's buses every single day. The most iconic bus is the double-decker, rear-doored Routemaster. It was replaced in 2005 by more modern versions, but there are quite a few still on display and running on popular tourist routes and making everyone feel nostalgic. Ahhh.

An old-fashioned Routemaster

ALL ABOARD THE GHOST BUS

A phantom number 7 ghost bus is said to appear in the middle of the night in Cambridge Gardens, with no driver and no lights. Spooky!

ROCKING IT IN RED

Before 1907, there were lots of different colored buses run by different companies. The London General Omnibus Company painted theirs red to stand out and they soon became the biggest bus operator in town.

Daredevil motorcycle stunt riders love to jump over London double-decker buses. Stunt star Eddie Kidd once jumped over 14!

TURN OVER TO MAKE

This bus build is cute as a button. All together now: "The wheels on the bus go round and round...."

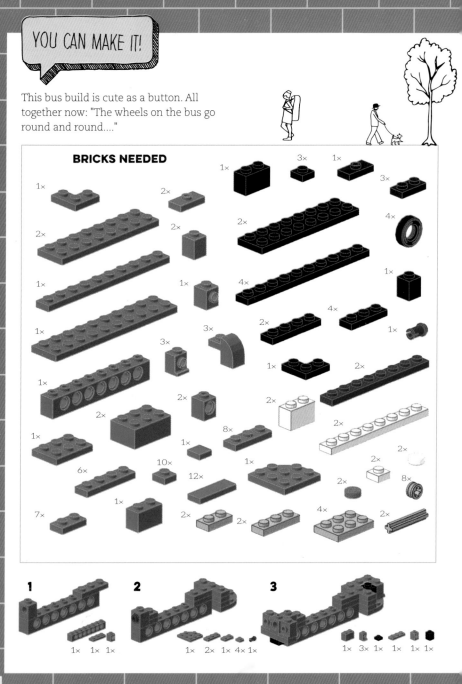

BRICKS NEEDED

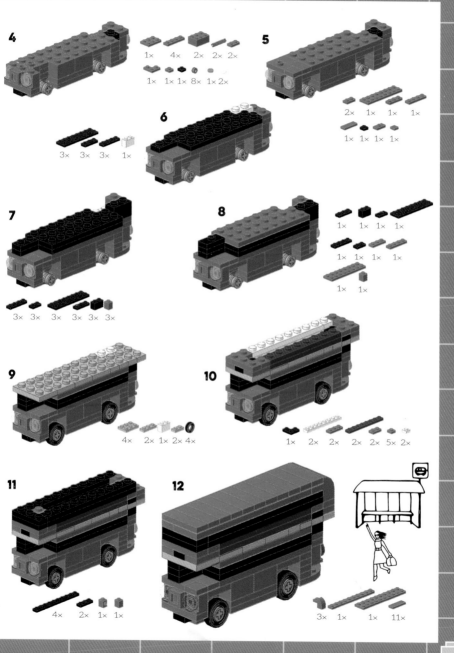

4

1× 4× 2× 2× 2×

1× 1× 1× 8× 1× 2×

5

2× 1× 1× 1×

1× 1× 1× 1×

6

3× 3× 3× 1×

7

3× 3× 3× 3× 3× 3×

8

1× 1× 1× 1×

1× 1× 1× 1×

1× 1×

9

4× 2× 1× 2× 4×

10

1× 2× 2× 2× 2× 5× 2×

11

4× 2× 1× 1×

12

3× 1× 1× 11×

ABBEY ROAD

There are at least
10 Abbey Roads
across London.

Cameras at the ready! Visitors from across the globe stride across the Abbey Road crosswalk all day long while their friends take photos—and all because of a world-famous supergroup. The Beatles posed here for the cover of their bestselling *Abbey Road* album, released in 1969.

The Beatles crossing Abbey Road

GEORGE

PAUL

RINGO

JOHN

RAT

106

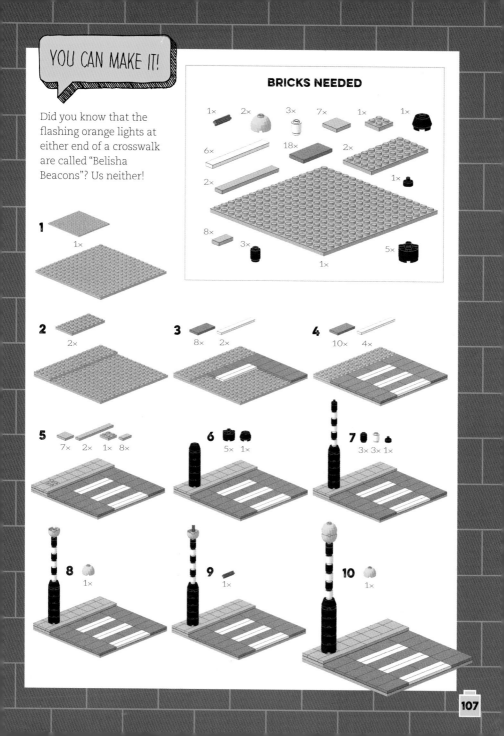

YOU CAN MAKE IT!

Did you know that the flashing orange lights at either end of a crosswalk are called "Belisha Beacons"? Us neither!

BRICKS NEEDED

1× 2× 3× 7× 1× 1×
6× 18× 2×
2× 1×
8×
3× 5×
1×

1
1×

2
2×

3
8× 2×

4
10× 4×

5
7× 2× 1× 8×

6
5× 1×

7
3× 3× 1×

8
1×

9
1×

10
1×

THE ORBIT

London is the only world city to host the Olympics three times—in 1908, 1948, and 2012. Nine hundred million people worldwide tuned into the 2012 opening ceremony in East London's Olympic Park. The Orbit sculpture was designed by famous architect Sir Anish Kapoor to mark the celebrations.

GOING FOR GOLD

Among the many Olympic records broken in 2012 the most celebrated was sprinter Usain Bolt's 9.63-second 100 meter marvel. Things were different in the first two London Olympics. The 1908 competition included tug-of-war, powerboat racing, and polo. The 1948 event included artistic events as well as sporting ones.

Bolt crossing the finishing line

Ride the slide

The twisting, turning steel structure is held together by 35,000 bolts. Brave visitors can ride the hair-raising slide from the top—it was designed by artist Carsten Höller.

CORKSCREWS TO SOLID GROUND IN JUST 40 SECONDS.

THE WORLD'S LONGEST AND TALLEST SLIDE

THRILL SEEKERS CAN ABSEIL OFF THE ORBIT!

The Orbit was sponsored by ArcelorMittal, the world's largest steel company. It is made from recycled steel.

Lord's Cricket Ground

Lord's Cricket Ground is England's "home of cricket." The country's most important Test matches take place here and cricket buffs (often in fancy dress!) join them for long lazy days listening to the sound of leather on willow.

ASHES TO ASHES

When the England cricket team first lost on home soil to Australia in 1882, a newspaper announced the death of English cricket. When the English team next went to Australia they were given a tiny urn representing "the Ashes", and the two teams still play a hotly contested series of games for the Ashes to this day. The Ashes urn is sacred to cricket fans and is a symbol of the rivalry between the two countries.

YOU CAN MAKE IT!

Dibbly-dobbly, dolly catch and donkey drop…these are just a few quirky cricket terms! Luckily you don't have to be able to speak cricket to make this model.

BRICKS NEEDED

43×   2×   1×   2×

3×

1×

1

2   1×   2×

3   18×

4   18×   3×

×2

5   4×   2×

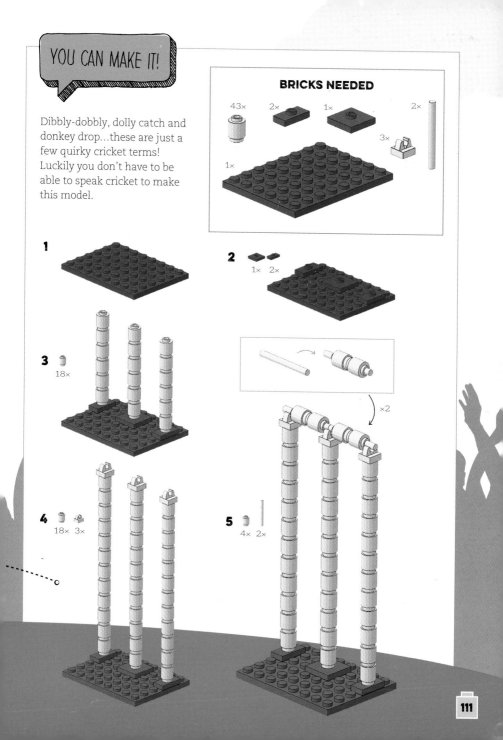

Wimbledon

London may be a built-up city, but it's got plenty of room for sport. One of the top tennis competitions on the planet is played right here in the leafy suburb of Wimbledon. Nowadays it's watched by around 1.2 billion TV viewers, but the event began way back in 1877, long before TV, making it the world's oldest tennis tournament.

AROUND 750 SCHOOL CHILDREN APPLY FOR THE POSITION OF BALL GIRL AND BALL BOY.

54,250 PRE-TESTED TENNIS BALLS ARE USED DURING THE TOURNAMENT.

WIMBLEDON IN NUMBERS

$3.1 (£2.2) million prize money for singles champions

11 hours 5 minutes played during the longest match (John Isner vs Nicolas Mahut, 2010)

500,000 spectators in total

166,000 serving of strawberries

2,199 gallons (10,000 liters) of cream

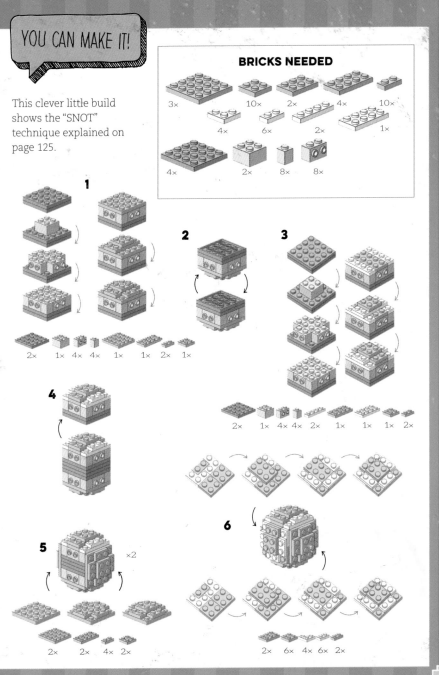

YOU CAN MAKE IT!

This clever little build shows the "SNOT" technique explained on page 125.

BRICKS NEEDED

3× 10× 2× 4× 10×

4× 6× 2× 1×

4× 2× 8× 8×

1

2× 1× 4× 4× 1× 1× 2× 1×

2

3

2× 1× 4× 4× 2× 1× 1× 1× 2×

4

5 ×2

2× 2× 4× 2×

6

2× 6× 4× 6× 2×

Camden Lock

Be prepared for an explosion of color, sound and activity if you visit Camden. This north London neighborhood is best known for its colorful, bohemian residents and rock-and-roll music venues. Famous singer Amy Winehouse, with her signature "beehive" hair-do, was one of its most famous residents.

Colorful Camden

PIRATE CASTLE

Aharrr! There's a pirate castle in the heart of London, and no mistake, Cap'n! It's a sailing club and theater for children at Camden Lock, and it all began in 1966. Kindly local Lord St. David founded the club for mini-pirates to learn to sail and in return they nicknamed him Peg-leg. His cracking canal-based charity continues today in its mock canalside castle.

Alongside Camden Lock—a device for lowering and raising the level of the Regent's Canal—are several huge markets where you can enjoy the spicy scent of international foods and shop for far-out items—from cyberpunk shoes to juggling balls, and ice cream frozen using liquid nitrogen!

REGENT'S CANAL

Canals once played a vital role in transporting goods across the capital. The Regent's Canal is a 9 mile (14.5km) ribbon of water that runs all the way from Little Venice to the River Thames. The stretch from Little Venice to Camden Town passes beautiful Regent's Park and London Zoo, as well as grand villas designed by architect John Nash.

Granary Square

Behind King's Cross Station, Granary Square is at the heart of a major canal-side redevelopment once full of abandoned warehouses. It has a mesmerizing fountain with 1,080 colorfully-lit water jets, which pulse and dance. On hot days the whole area becomes a busy urban beach.

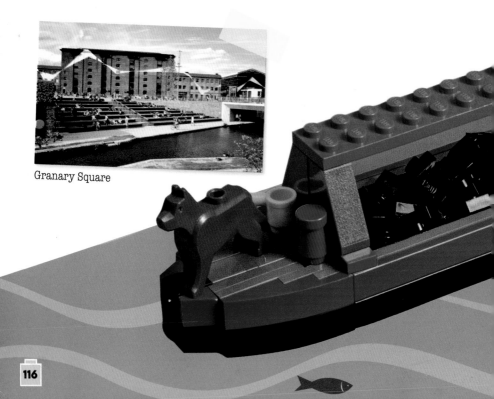

Granary Square

A longboat on Regent's Canal

A HOT TUB WITH A DIFFERENCE

HotTug is the world's first floating hot tub. A cozy fire keeps its waters warm while visitors explore the Regent's Canal nose-to-beak with local ducks.

TURN OVER TO MAKE

CANAL BOAT

This cute model is based on a traditional narrowboat design.

BRICKS NEEDED

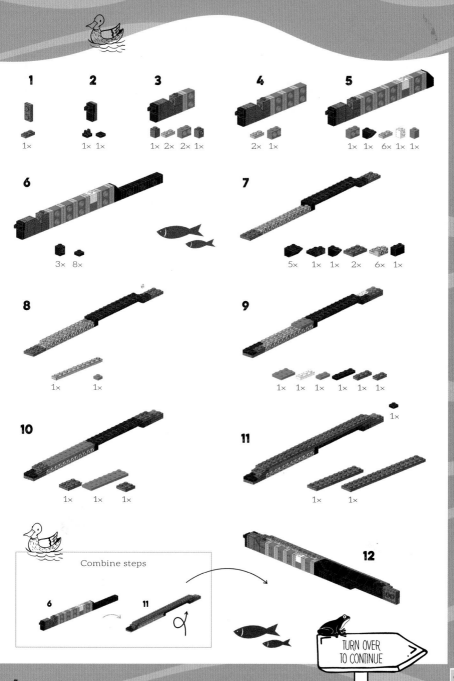

1
1×

2
1× 1×

3
1× 2× 2× 1×

4
2× 1×

5
1× 1× 6× 1× 1×

6
3× 8×

7
5× 1× 1× 2× 6× 1×

8
1× 1×

9
1× 1× 1× 1× 1× 1×
1×

10
1× 1× 1×

11
1× 1×

Combine steps

6

11

12

TURN OVER TO CONTINUE

CANAL BOAT

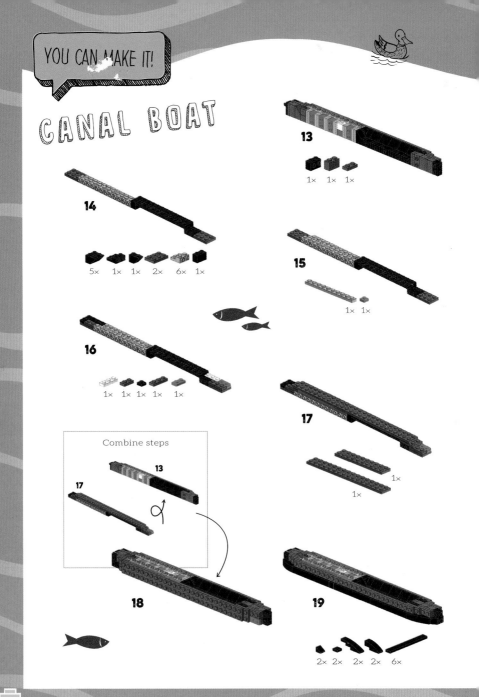

13

1× 1× 1×

14

5× 1× 1× 2× 6× 1×

15

1× 1×

16

1× 1× 1× 1× 1×

17

1×

1×

Combine steps

13

17

18

19

2× 2× 2× 2× 6×

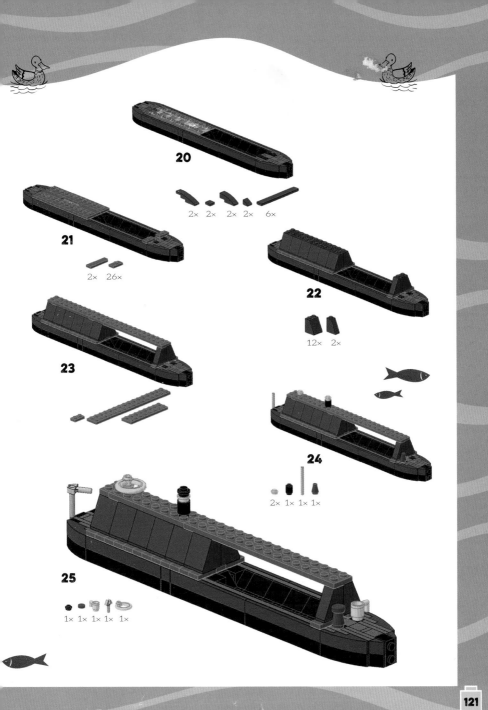

20

2× 2× 2× 2× 6×

21

2× 26×

22

12× 2×

23

24

2× 1× 1× 1×

25

1× 1× 1× 1× 1×

Sherlock Holmes, the world-famous detective, lived at 221b Baker Street. Inside, the rooms are filled with his Victorian belongings, including his hat, pipes, violin, and equipment for solving mysteries.

But hold on a minute...

Holmes was an imaginary character in books written by Sir Arthur Conan Doyle. More than a few fans of the classic detective novels make the trek to this house museum to be greeted by costumed staff.

The Sherlock Holmes Museum

HOLMES DIDN'T REALLY WEAR A DEERSTALKER HAT THAT MUCH!

221B BAKER ST

For years there was a dispute over this famous address, which was actually occupied by Abbey National Bank. A secretary even had the job of responding to fan mail. When the bank moved out, the Royal Mail recognized the museum's right to receive post addressed to Sherlock Holmes.

THE MUSEUM IS ACTUALLY AT NUMBER 239.

YOU CAN MAKE IT!

This full-size magnifying glass model is the perfect accessory for any wannabe detective. Just follow the clues!

BRICKS NEEDED

1×
4×
4×
4×
2×
12×
2×
8×
2×
2×
3×
1×
9×
1×
4×

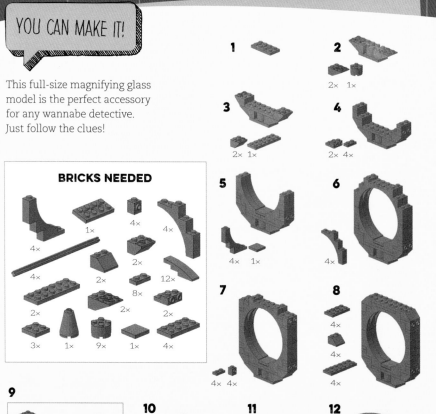

1

2
2× 1×

3
2× 1×

4
2× 4×

5
4× 1×

6
4×

7
4× 4×

8
4×
4×
4×

9
3×
12×
3×

10
1×

11
8×

12
1×

123

10 most useful bricks

These are the most exciting bricks in LEGO®
building. No matter how many of them you
have, there will never quite be enough!

1

2×4 BRICK

The oldest brick
around, this is a
classic. Strong, and
great for adding
structure to
something fragile.

2

1×2 BRACKET

Introduced in 2012,
and so useful! These
pieces help where
other brackets can't
and add real strength
to your models.

3

1×1×⅔ SLOPE
(or "cheese" slope)

A great piece
that gives models
a smooth, modern
look. Useful for
buildings, vehicles,
and animals.

4

1×1 ROUND PLATE
WITH HOLE

These parts
are perfect for
anchoring rods.

5

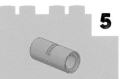

TECHNIC PIN JOINER

Structural steelwork
is very important in
architecture and
these pieces joined
together are just the
right shape.

6

1×4 PLATE HINGE

Small but strong
hinges that let you
choose the exact
angle for the pieces
of your creation.

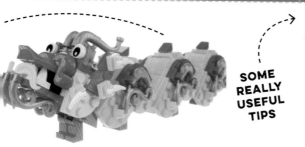

SOME REALLY USEFUL TIPS

BUILD TIPS

BRICKS & PLATES

One LEGO® brick is equal in height to three LEGO® plates. Plates give models more strength (they make great floors), and can incorporate more color variety and detail in the same space as a brick (see below).

3 = 1 Brick

"SNOT"

It stands for "Studs Not On Top"—this is a method of turning bricks or plates sideways to make it possible to create quite an accurate curve by turning half of the plates sideways. (see below).

7

1×1 "HEADLIGHT" BRICK

The original "Studs Not On Top" (SNOT) brick, used for headlights on millions of cars. Its geometry is actually very clever.

8

1×1 BRICK WITH A STUD ON ONE SIDE

These bricks give you a simple way of attaching a plate to the side of a brick. They are used for details or to add a special brick in an unexpected way.

7

1×2 PLATE WITH ONE STUD

(or "jumper")
When two studs are just too much! Jumpers offset the fine details.

10

1×1 BRICK WITH STUDS ON FOUR SIDES

These are fantastic for creating columns as they can point plates out in four directions.

LEGO® colors

With more than 140 LEGO® colors to choose from, which should you use?

Not all parts exist in all colors, and in fact some very common parts have never been made in some of the obvious colors.

Below and opposite is a guide to some, but not all, of the colors available, using their Bricklink names rather than the official LEGO® ones.

HOW TO FIND THE BRICKS YOU'LL NEED

No matter how many LEGO® bricks anyone has—it's never enough! You don't need to worry if you don't have exactly the same bricks as I've used for these models though. Just try building them with the bricks you have and your imagination!

If you do need to buy more bricks to build some of the models in this book then I've got some tips for you. Did you know you can buy bricks directly from www.lego.com? There is a special section on their online store, just for bricks. Here you can choose from a huge selection of bricks in all sorts of colors to help you build your city. If you're after something very different though, there are special websites allowing people like you to trade bricks? The two best known are www.bricklink.com and www.brickowl.com.

DARK PURPLE

TAN

TRANS-NEON ORANGE

TRANS-PINK

LIGHT YELLOW

DARK BROWN

PINK

TRANS-BLUE

TRANS-GREEN

OLIVE GREEN

PEARL GOLD

TRANS-LIGHT BLUE

CHROME SILVER

BRIGHT LIGHT BLUE

DARK FLESH

LIGHT PURPLE

AQUA

FUN RANGE OF COLOURS

TURQUOISE

SAND BLUE

PEARL LIGHT GRAY

PEARL BLACK

BRIGHT YELLOW

TRANS-RED

YELLOW

EARTH ORANGE

VIOLET

DARK RED

TRANS-PURPLE

TRANS-NEON GREEN

SAND GREEN

TRANS-DARK BLUE

TRANS-ORANGE

BRIGHT PINK

DARK BLUISH-GRAY

DARK ORANGE

TRANS-CLEAR

REDDISH BROWN

DARK TURQUOISE

TRANS-BLACK

DARK PINK

RED

PEARL SILVER

WHITE

LIGHT BLUISH-GRAY

GREEN

DARK AZURE

DARK TAN

PURPLE

MARBLED SILVER

ORANGE

MEDIUM DARK PINK

TRANS-YELLOW

BRIGHT GREEN

BLUE

LIGHT ORANGE

BRIGHT LIGHT YELLOW

DARK GREEN

LIME GREEN

DARK BLUE

MEDIUM BLUE

BLACK

MAERSK BLUE

Acknowledgments

I'd like to thank the other amazing builders who helped to contribute to this book. Rocco Buttliere had already created some amazing LEGO® models of London icons and as they say, there's no point in reinventing the wheel! In addition, my thanks to Alastair Disley, Kirsten Bedigan, Guy Bagley, Tim Johnson, Alex Mallinson, and Teresa Elsmore for being instrumental in bringing the book to life!

WE ALWAYS LIKE TO SAY THANK YOU!

ABOUT THE AUTHOR

Warren Elsmore is an artist in LEGO® bricks and a lifelong fan of LEGO®. He is based in Edinburgh, UK. He has been in love with the little bricks since the age of four and is now heavily involved in the LEGO® fan community. Since rediscovering his love of LEGO® at the age of 24, Warren has never looked back. In 2012, after 15 years in a successful IT career, he moved to working full time with LEGO® bricks and now helps many companies to realize their own dreams in plastic. He is the author of several LEGO® books and has organized several international LEGO® conventions.

Picture Credits

The publisher would like to thank the following for permission to reproduce copyright material

Alamy: p27, 32 (right) Steve Vidler/Mauritius Images GmbH; p27 Richard Bryant/Arcaid Images; p30 Edward Sumner-VIEW; p45 Peter Carroll; p66 Peter Barritt/robertharding; p76 Angelo Hornak; p80 eye35.pix; p106 Marc Tielemans; p.108 PCN Black; p117 Vikram Harish; p122 Gregory Wrona.

Shutterstock.com: p18 (left) Angelina Dimitrova; p18 (right) Dinko G Kyuchukov; p29 Peter Nadoiski; p32 (left) PriceM; p41 Bikeworldtravel; p48 Twocoms; p51 (top) Everett Historical; p51 (bottom) ricochet64; p60 Cedric Weber; p69 DrPhee; p71 Songquan Deng; p74 William Perugini; p96 alice-photo; p102 Chris Jenner; p114 Willy Barton; p116 Ron Ellis.

LEGO Builders: p10 Tate Modern © **Tim Johnson**; p6, 8, 12 Red Phone Box, p14 Globe Theatre, p8, 16 Bowler Hat, p19 Oxo Tower, p20 Battersea Power Station; p8, 23 10 Downing Street, p26 Palace of Westminster, p31 Tower of London, p8, 33 Crown Jewels Orb, p1, 3, 5, 8, 36 Raven, p8, 39 Stocks, p30 Union Jack, p8, 46 Coronation Chair, p49 Fourth Plinth, p4, 8, 52 City of London Dragon, p1, p61 Cleopatra's Needle, p63 Buckingham Palace, p8, 64 Queen's Guard, p68 BT Tower, p9, 71 British Museum, p76 London Monument, p9, 78 Fish and Chips, p81 Borough Market, p3, 9, 83 Food Truck, p89 Afternoon Tea, p9, 91 Chinese Dragon, p96 Covent Garden, p9, 98 Underground Train, p1, 4, 6, 7, 9, 103 Red Bus, p7, 9, 106 Abbey Road, p109 The Orbit, p9, 110 Wicket, p9, 112 Tennis Ball, p144 Camden Lock, p9, 116 Narrow Boat, p5, 9, 122 Magnifying Glass © **Warren Elsmore**; p5, 42 Westminster Abbey, p44 London Eye, p1, 74 The Shard © **Rocco Buttliere**; p66 St Pauls © **Alex M**.

While every effort has been made to credit photographers, The Bright Press would like to apologize should there have been any omissions or errors, and would be pleased to make the appropriate correction for future editions of the book.